This Coloring Book Belongs To:

_____

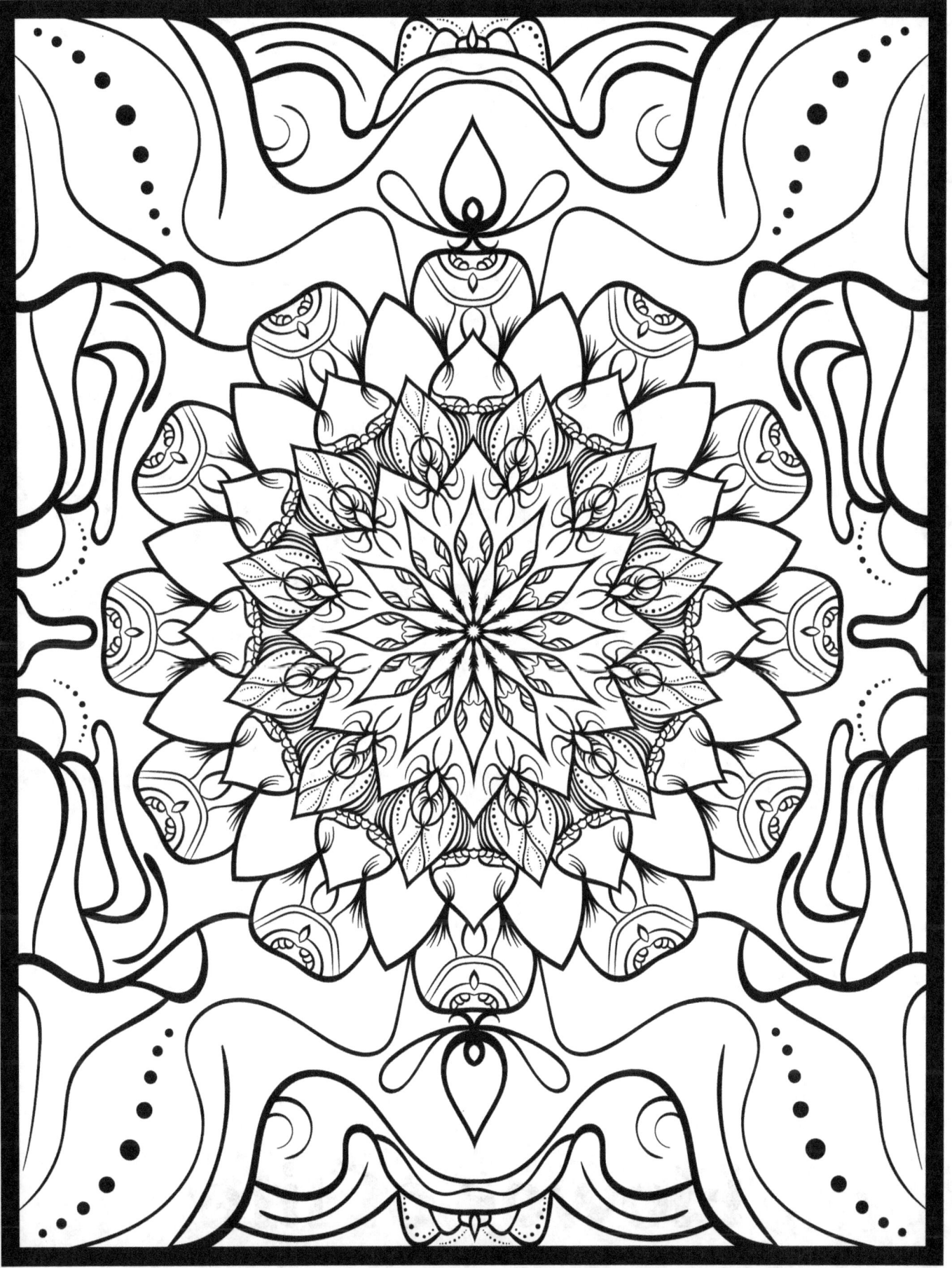

Flower of life

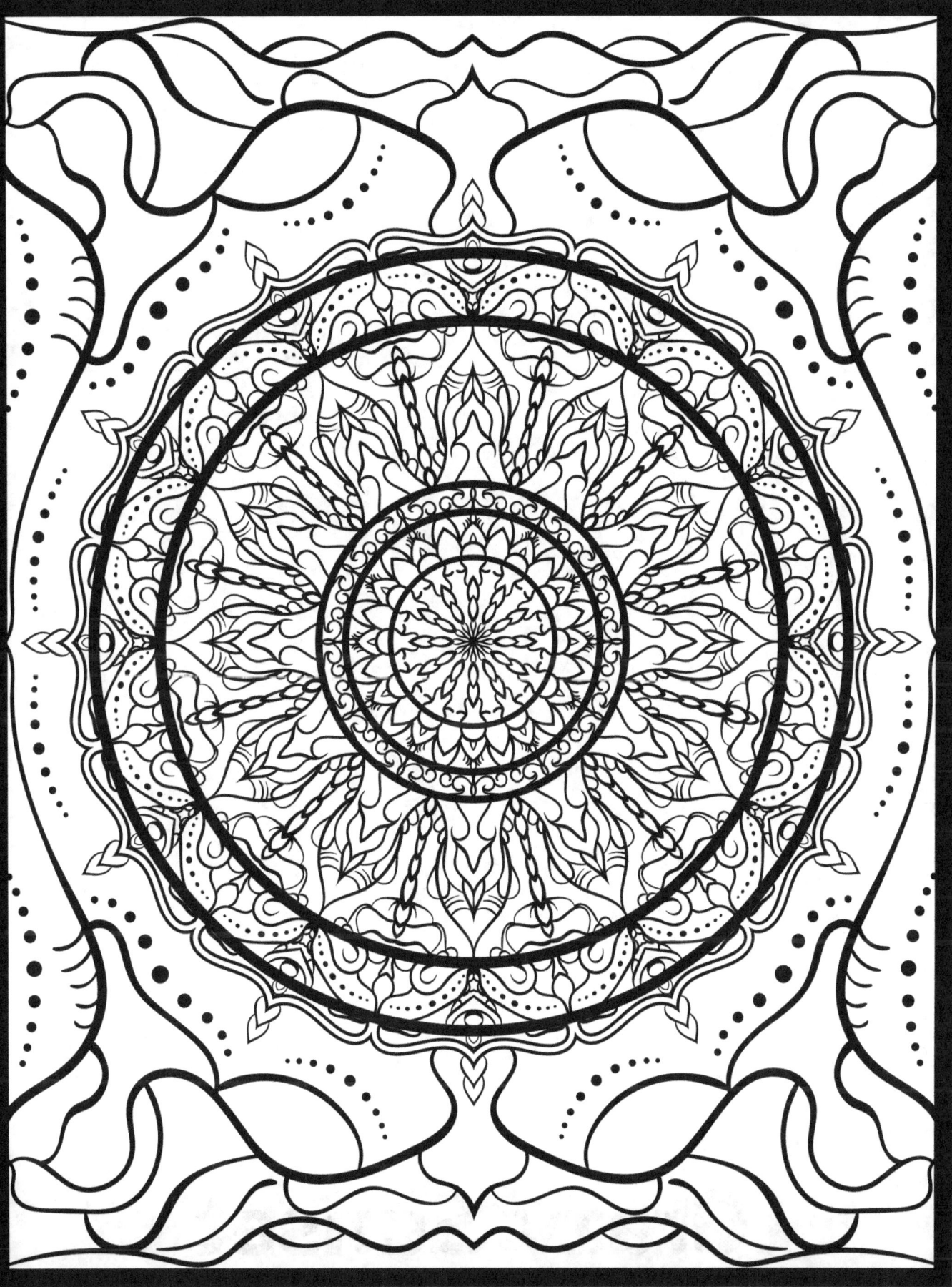

Crazy Sunset

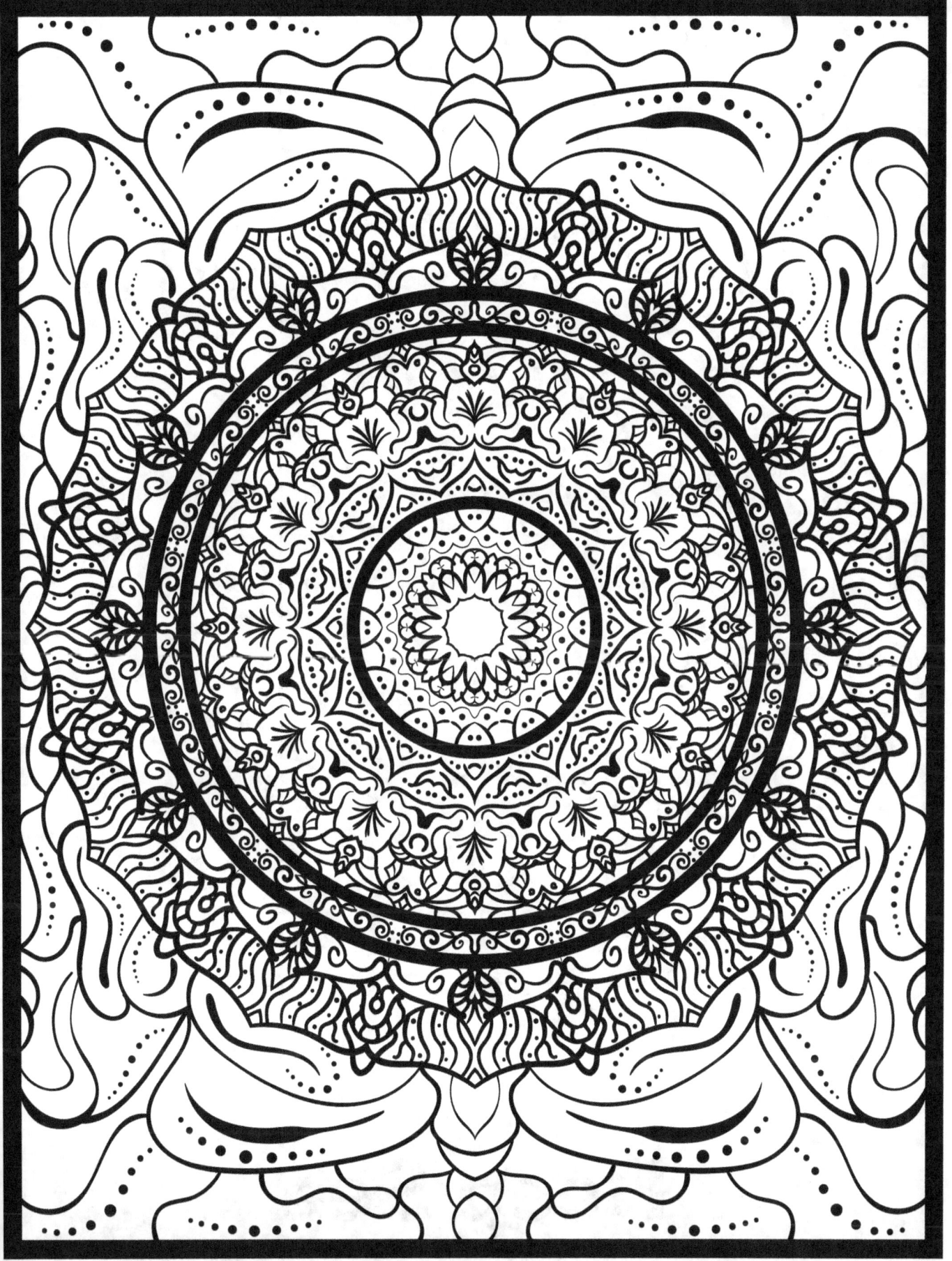

Deep Sea

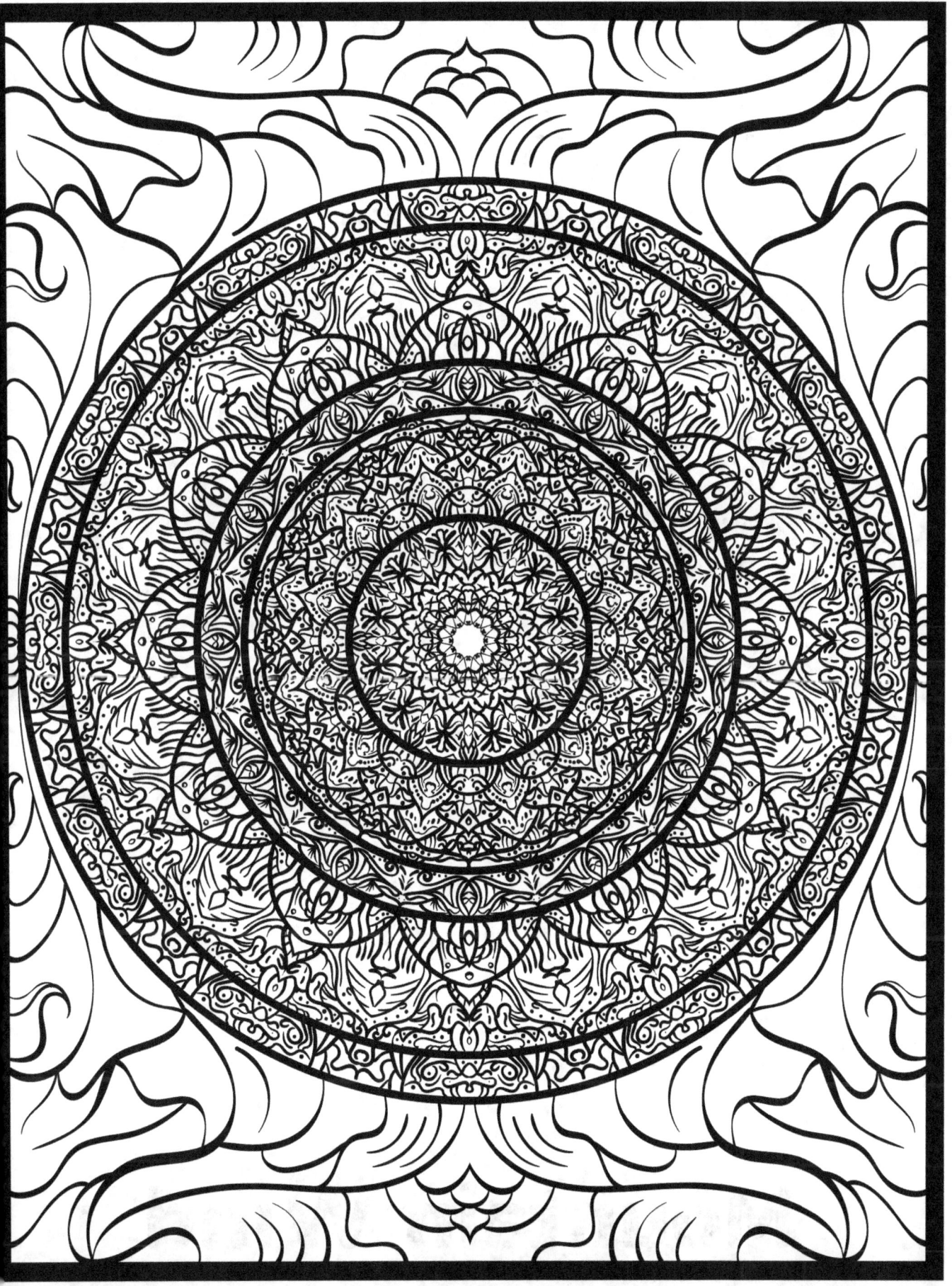

Mountain Wind

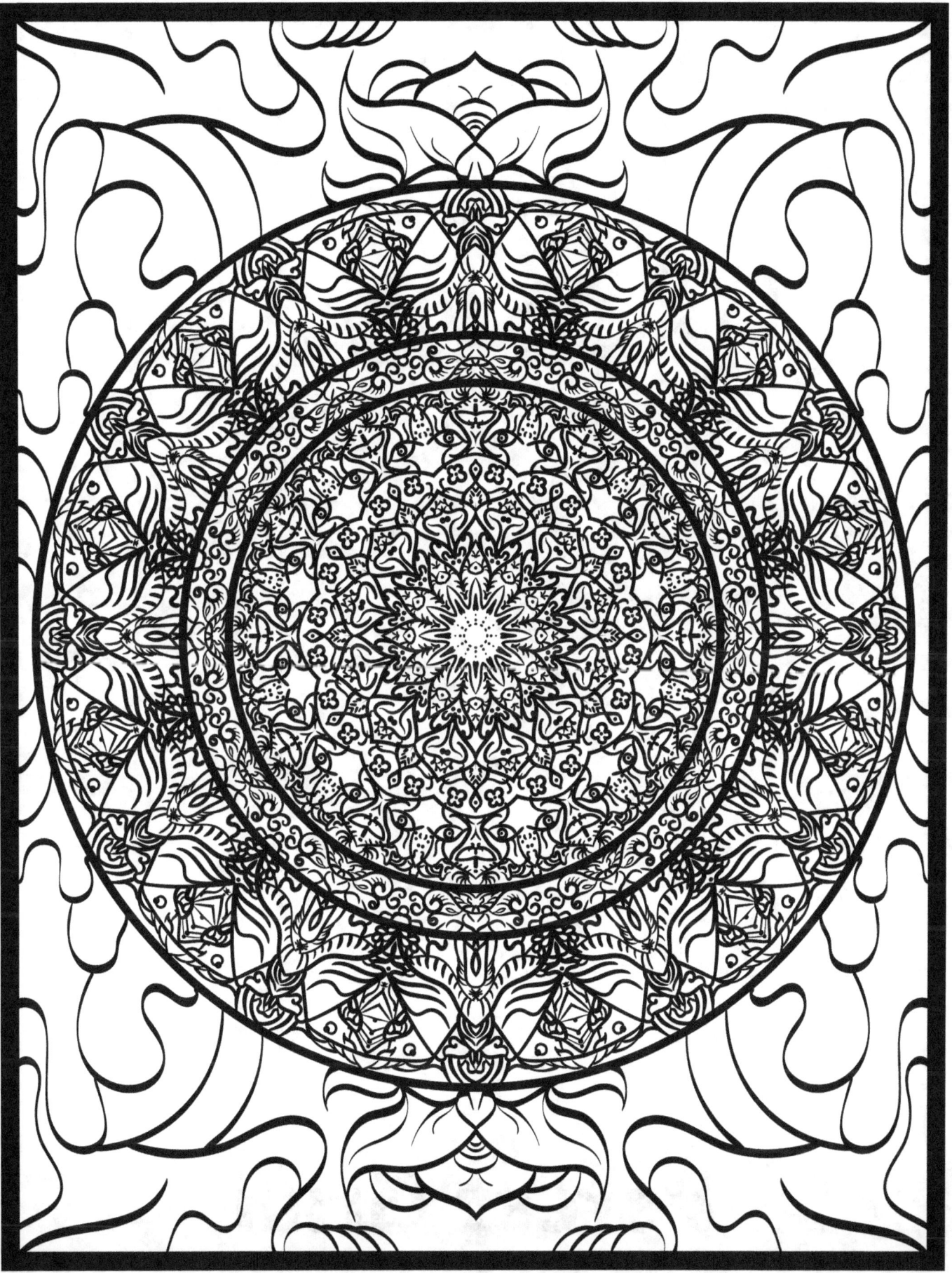

Forest Grial

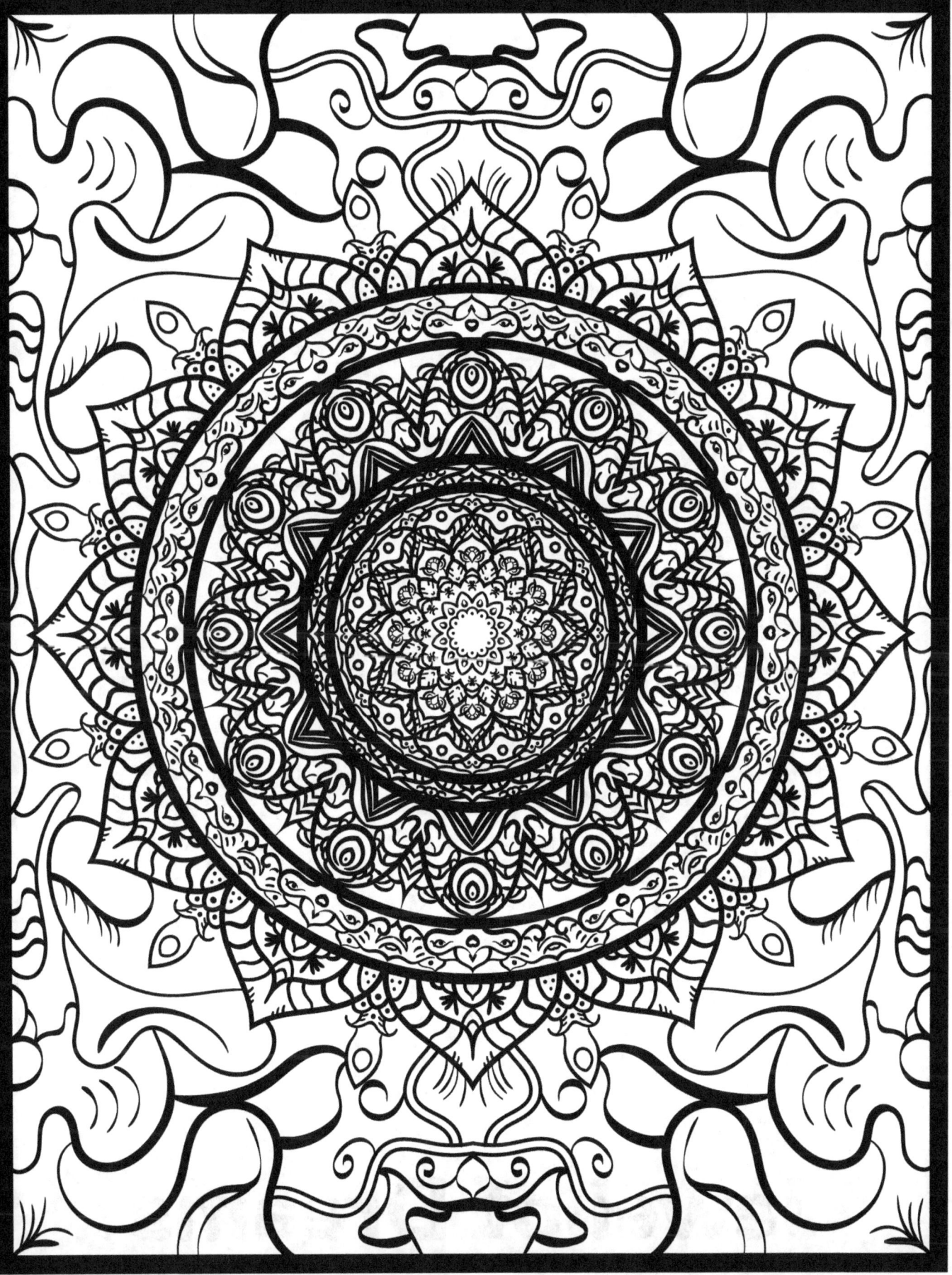

Jewel of Dreams

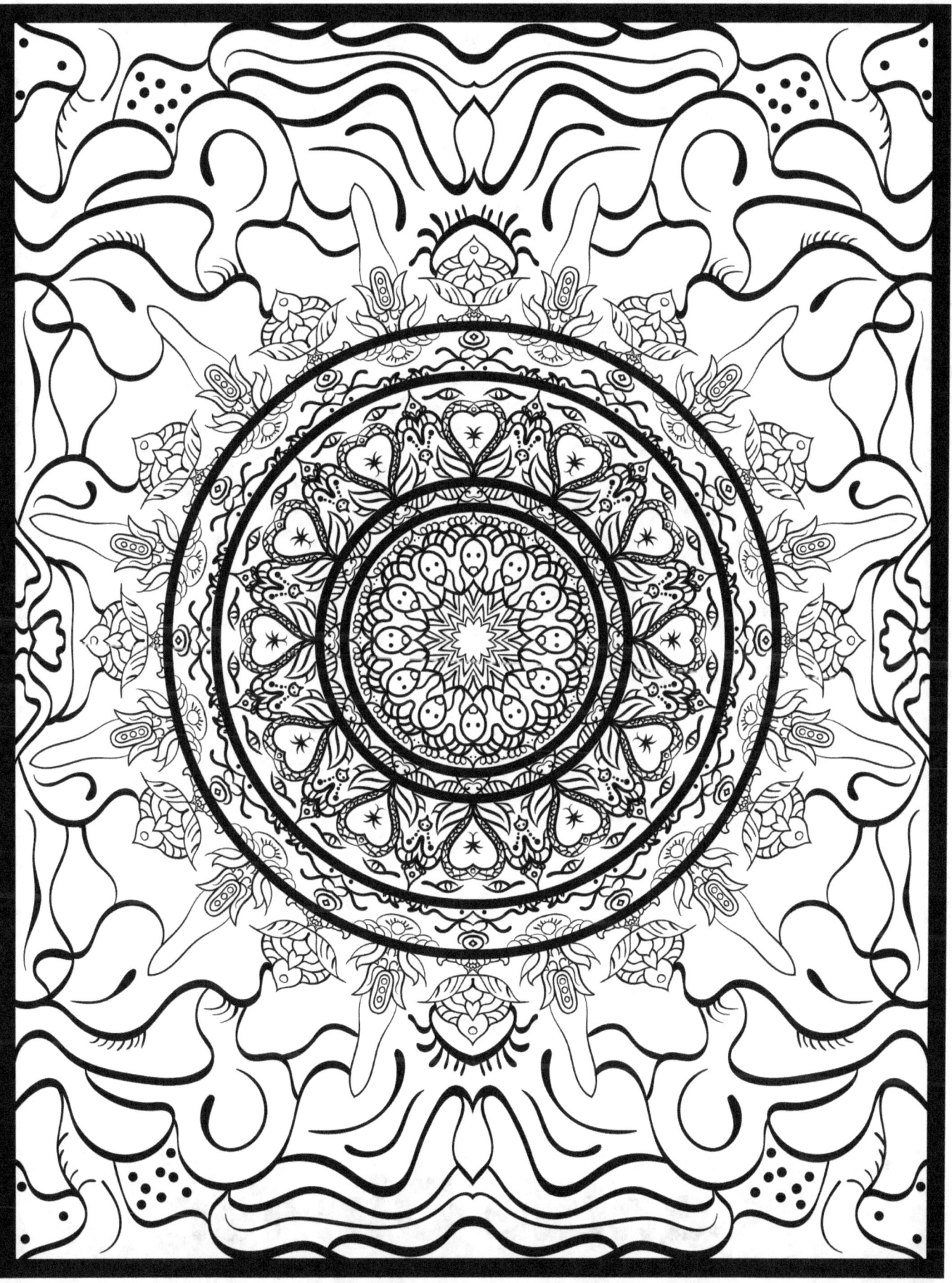

Candle Dinner

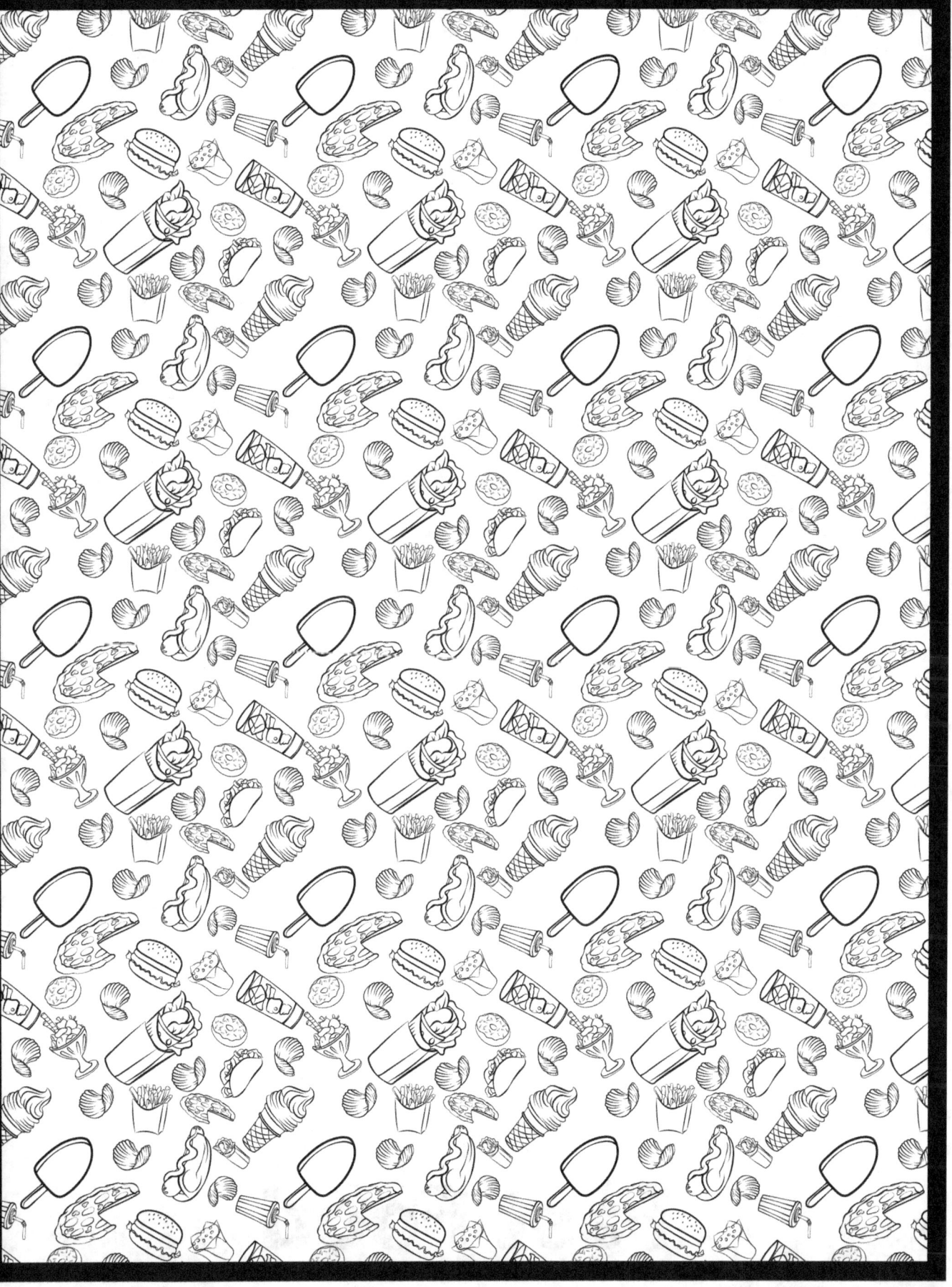

Fast Food

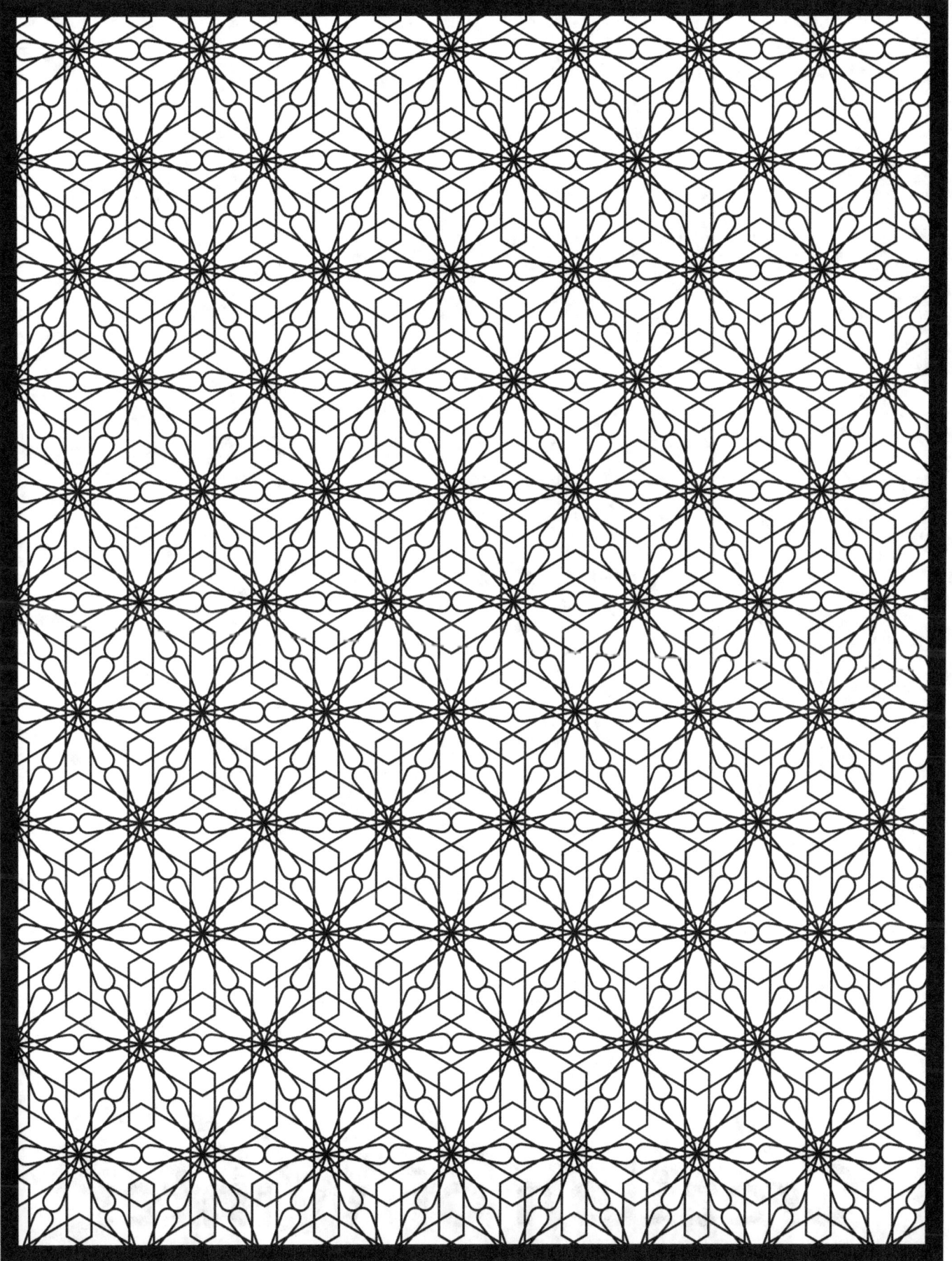

Creation of Winter

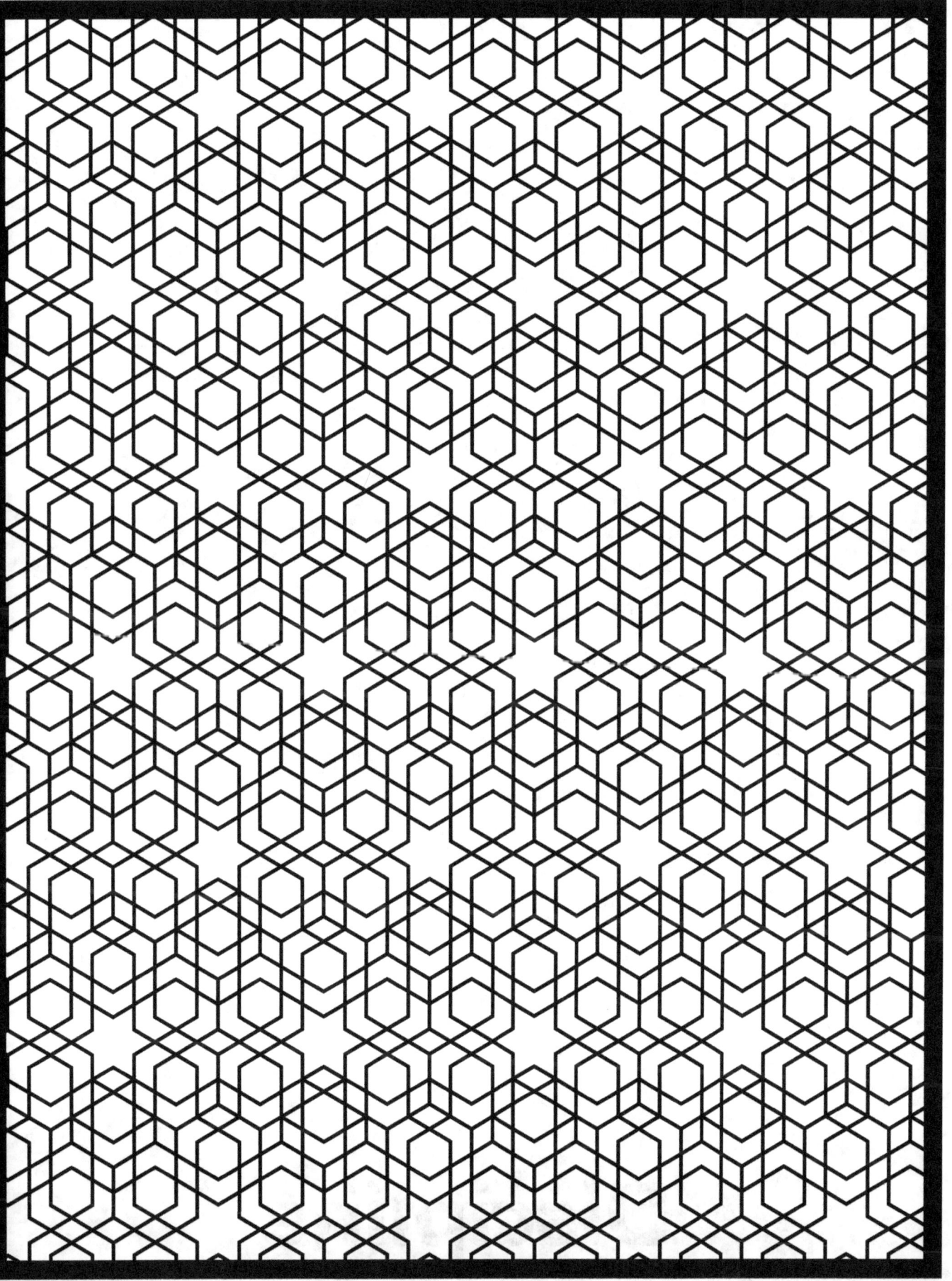

Discipline

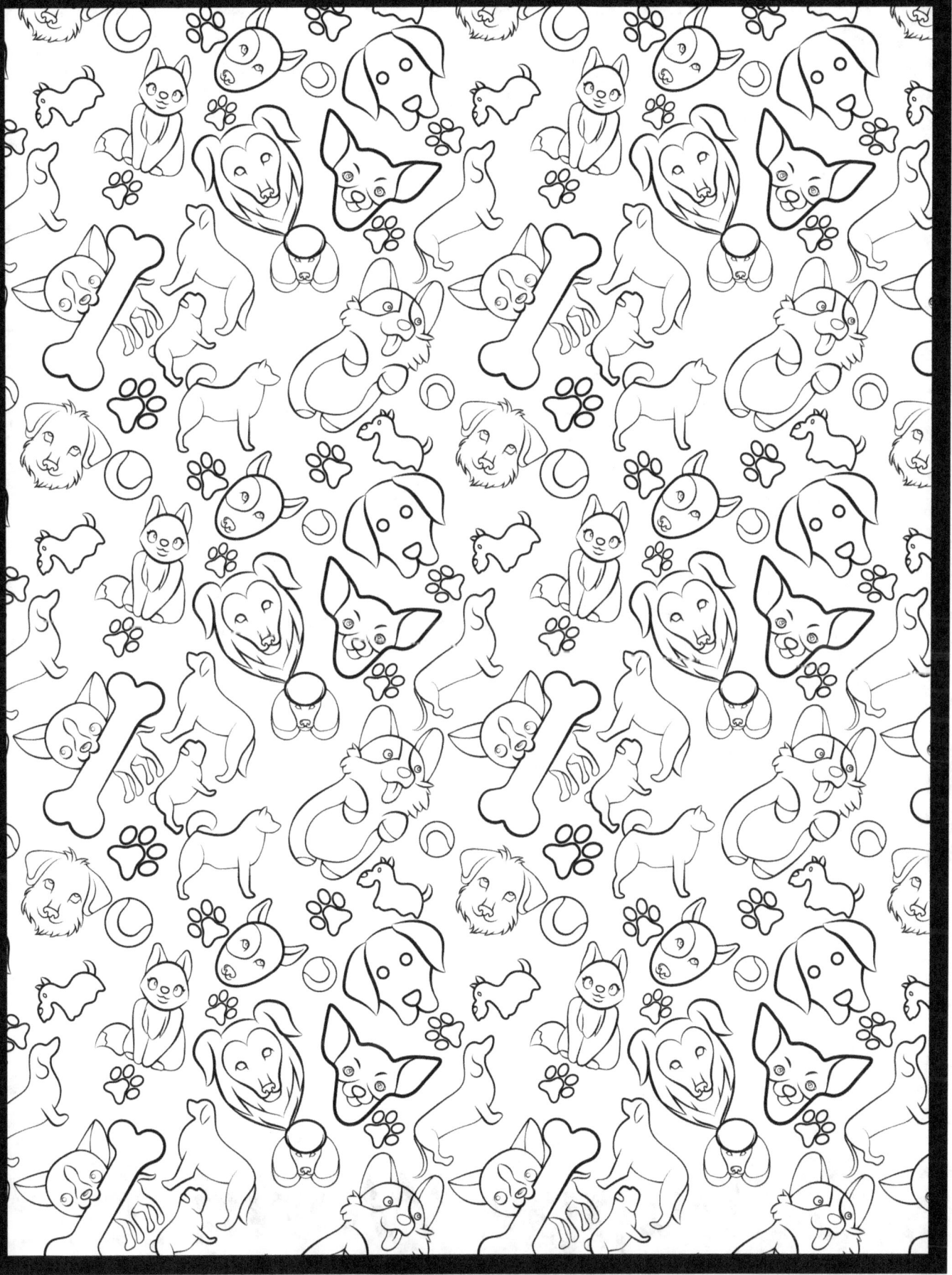

Puppy World

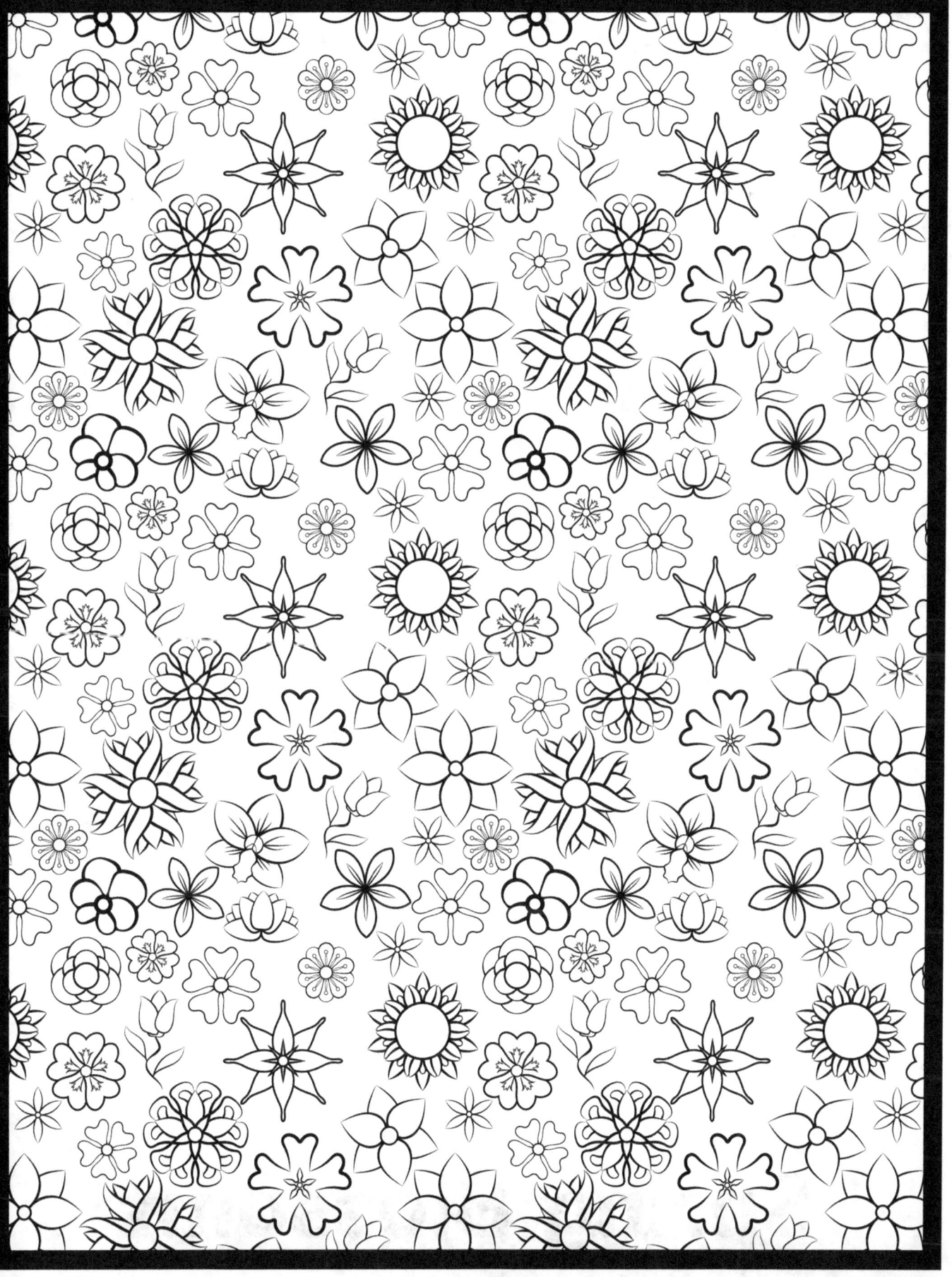

Spring Blossoms

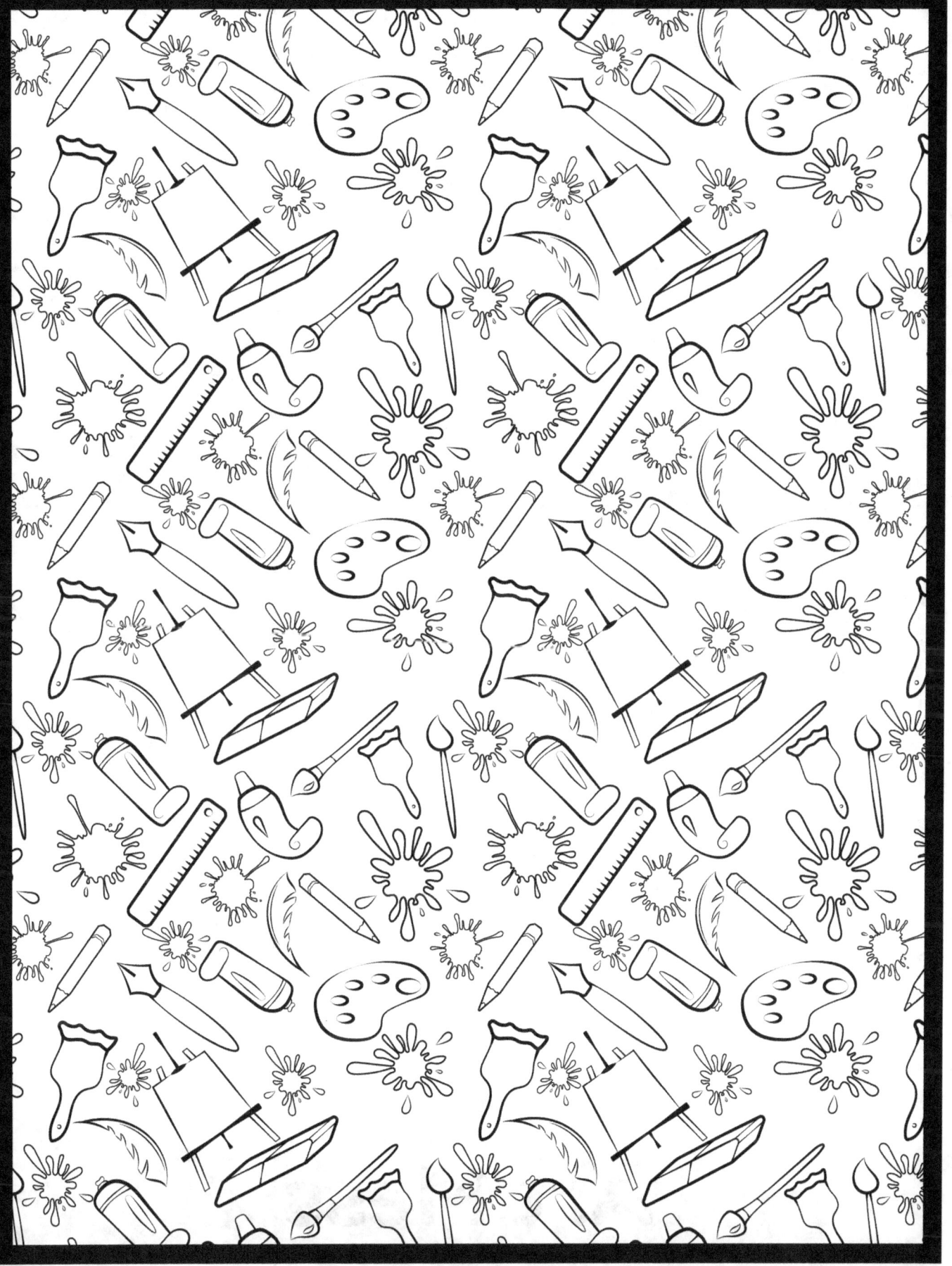

Art Mess

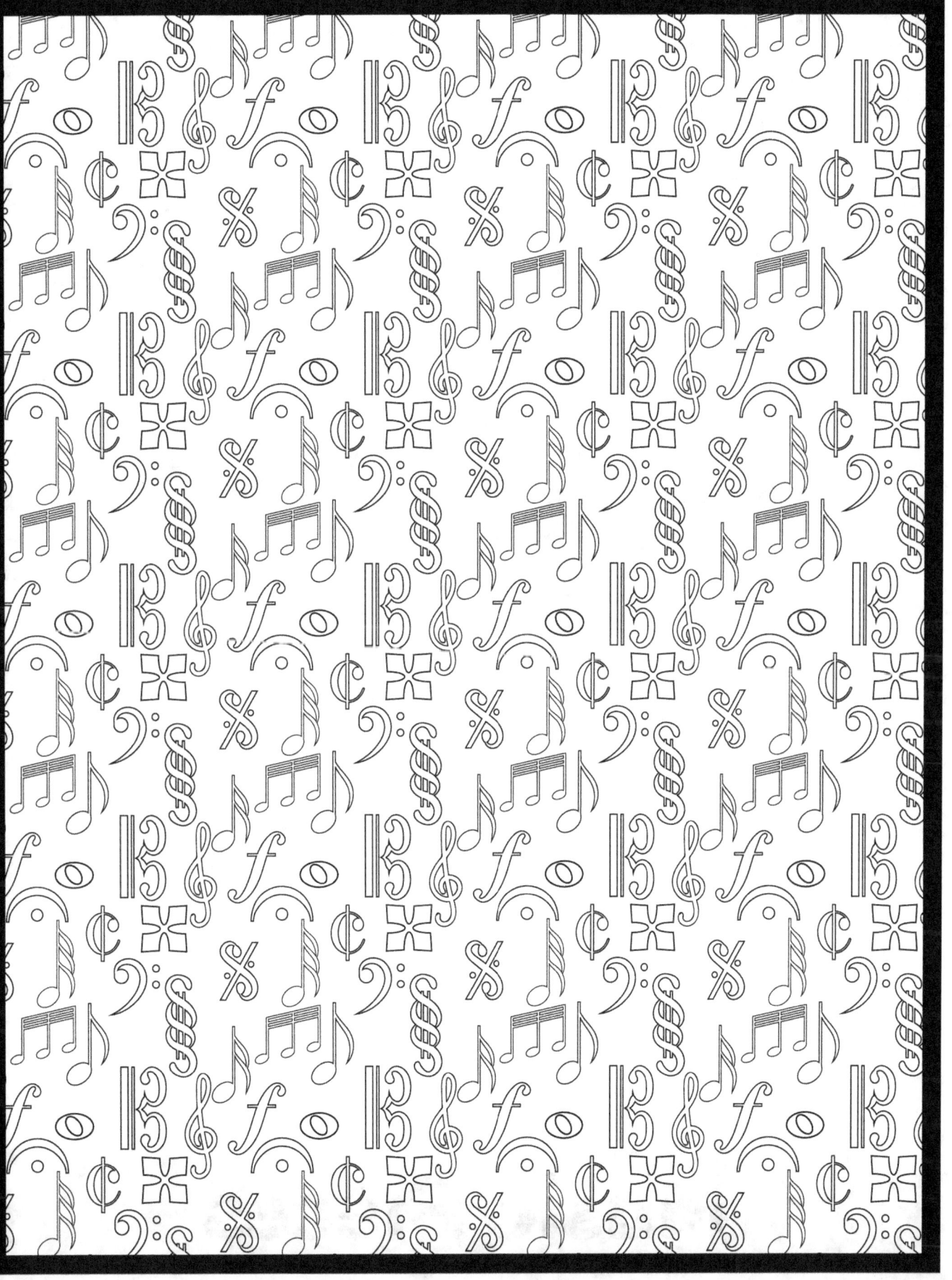

Music Pieces

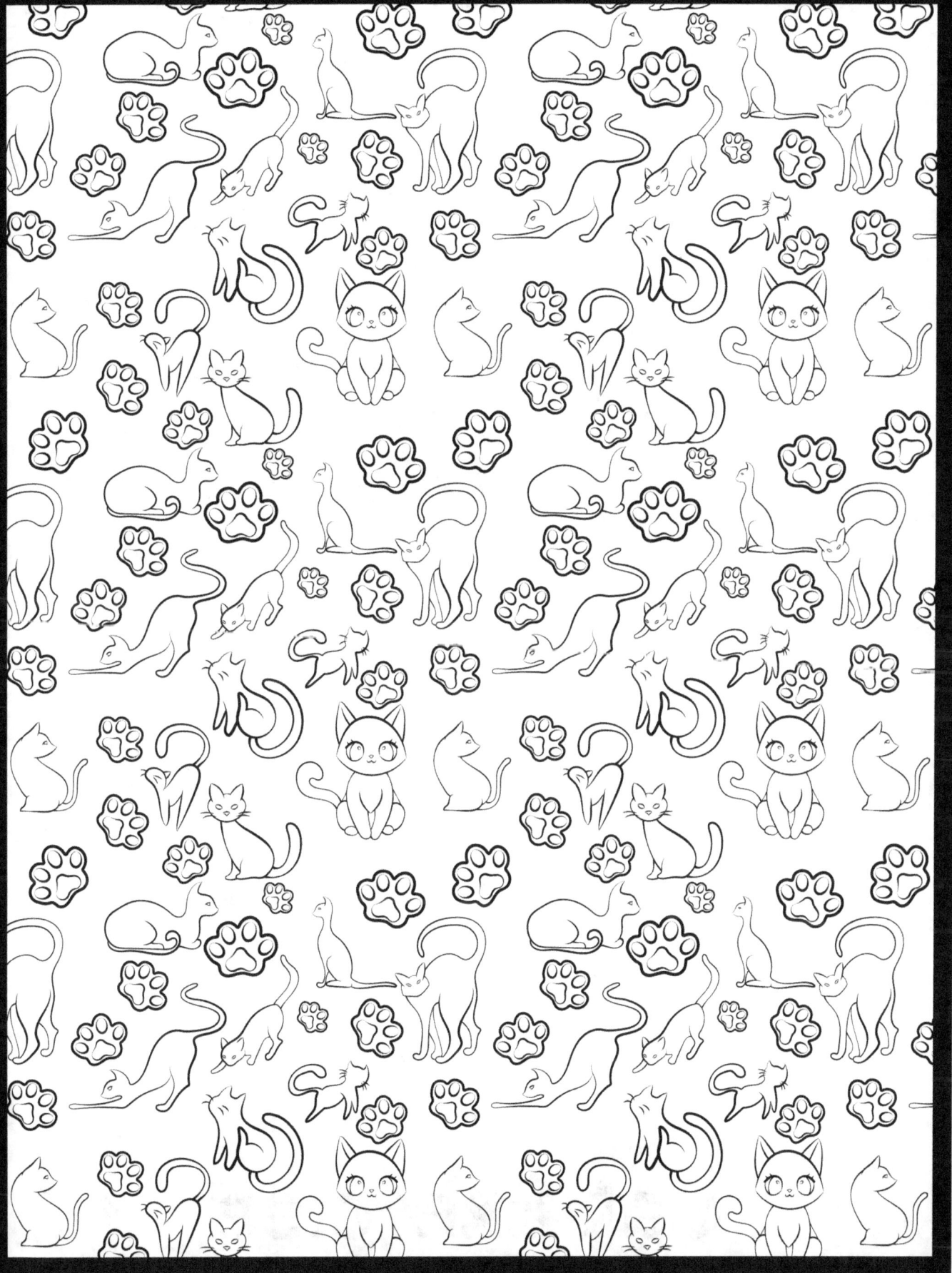

Cat Exercise

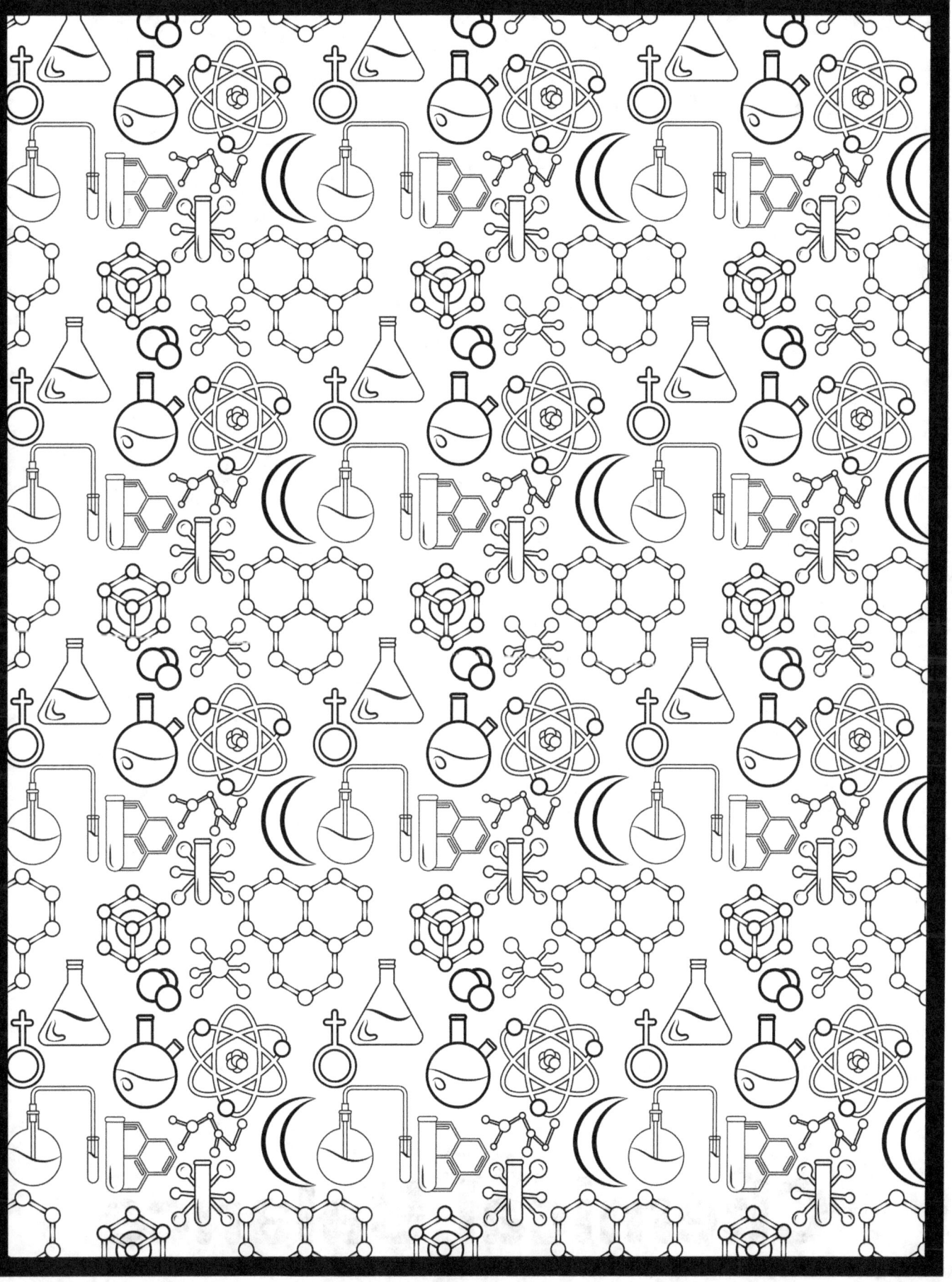

Chemical Balance

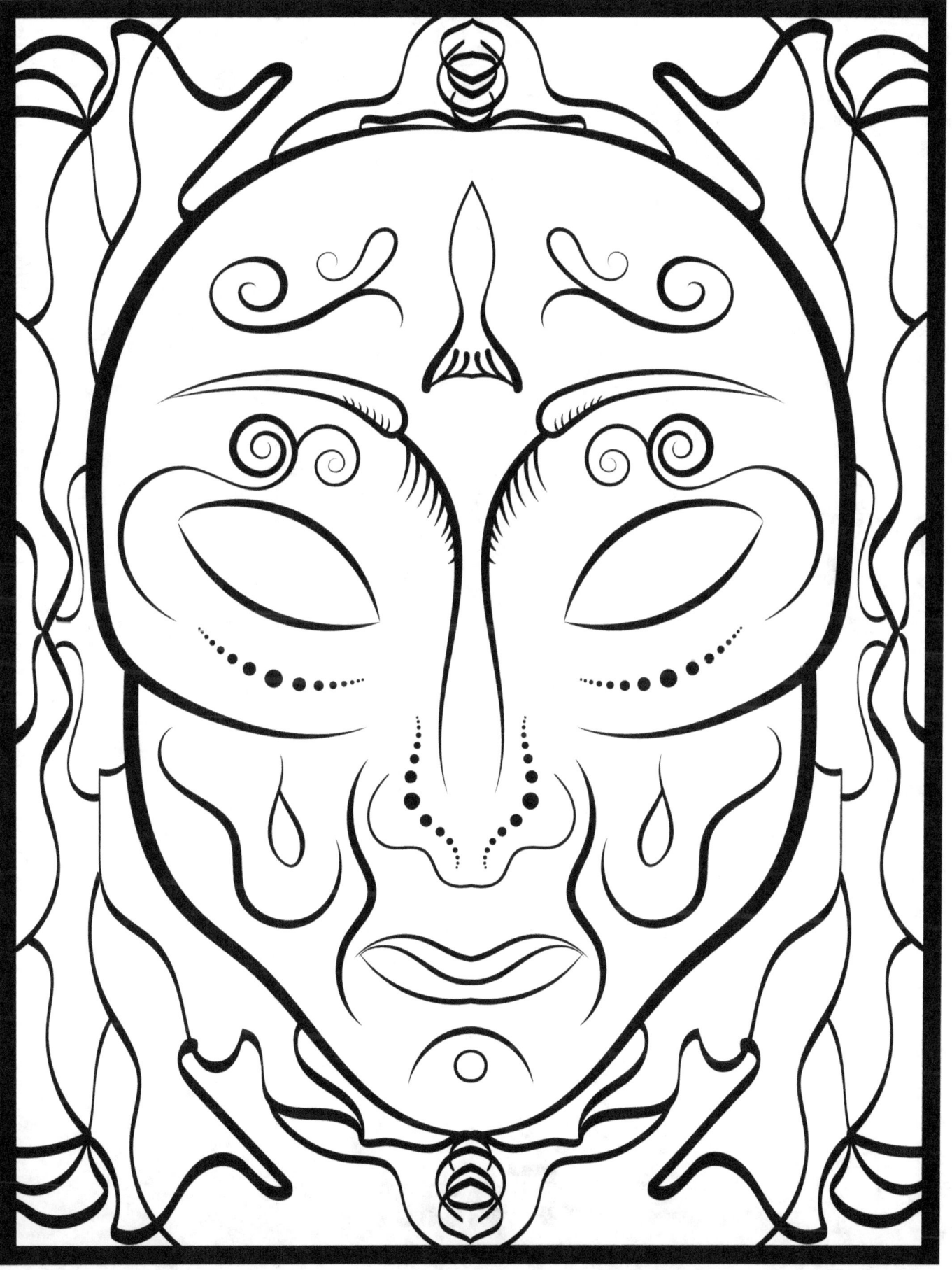

Fear

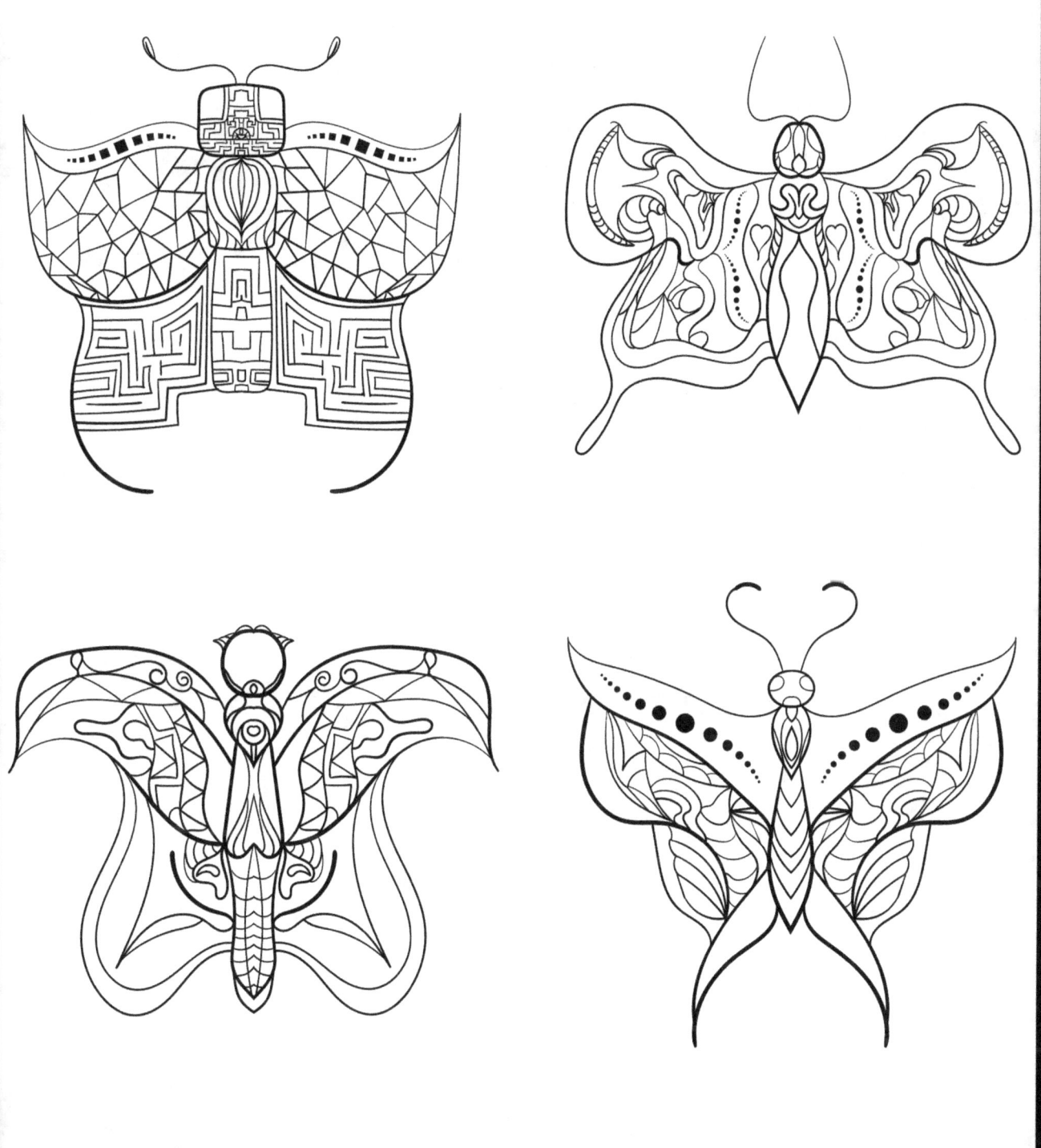

Seasons

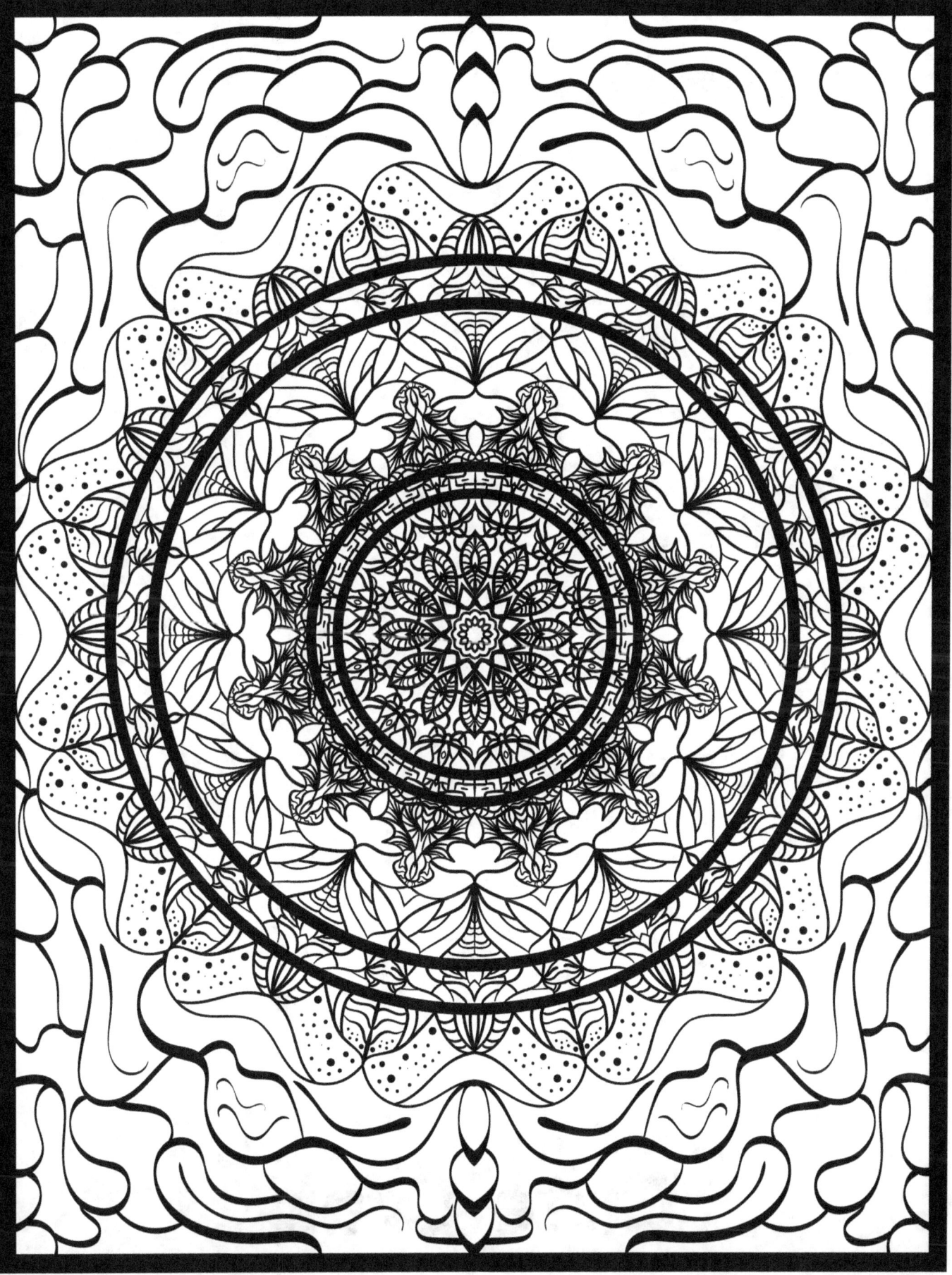

Cute Crab

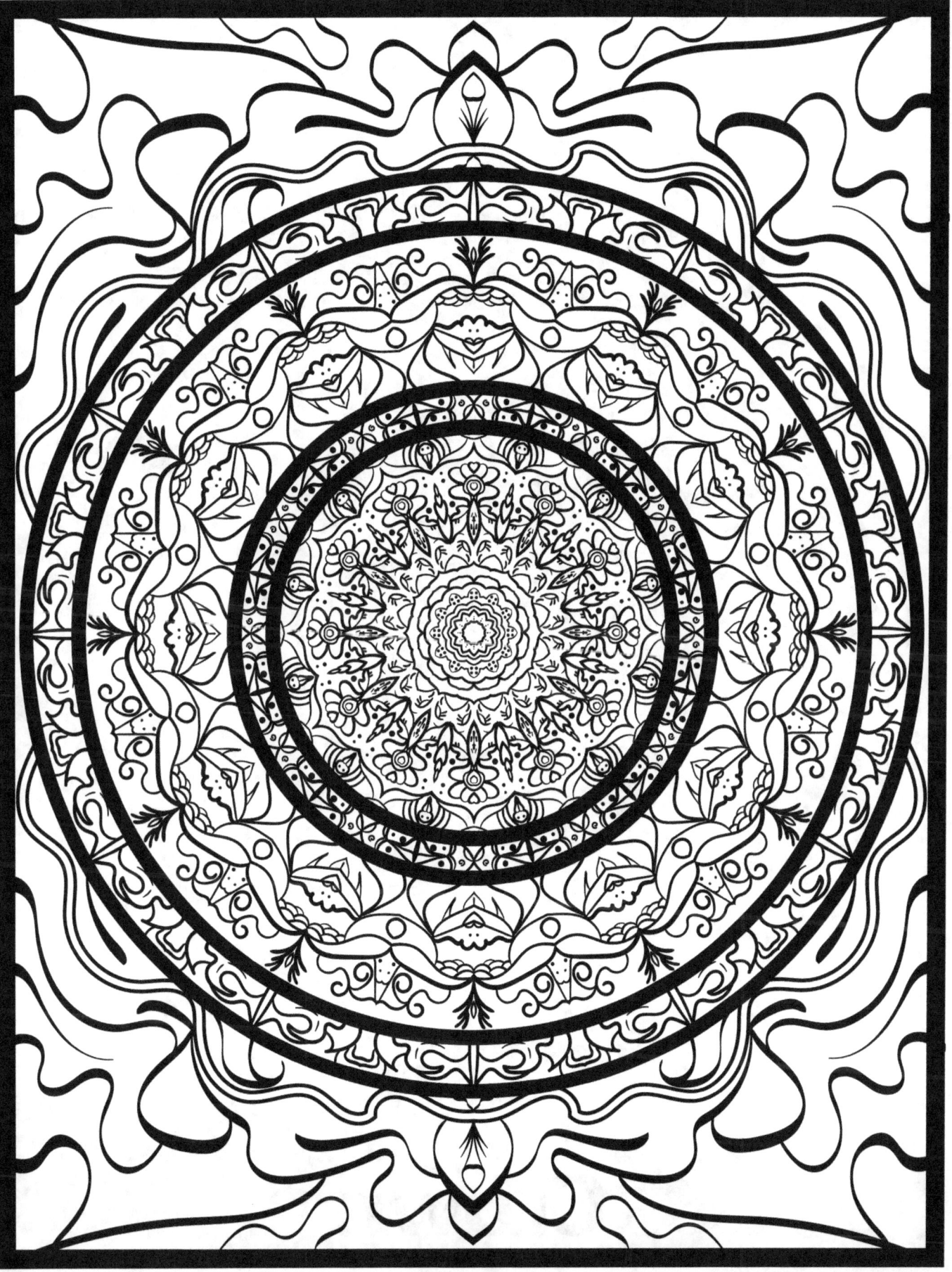

Crown

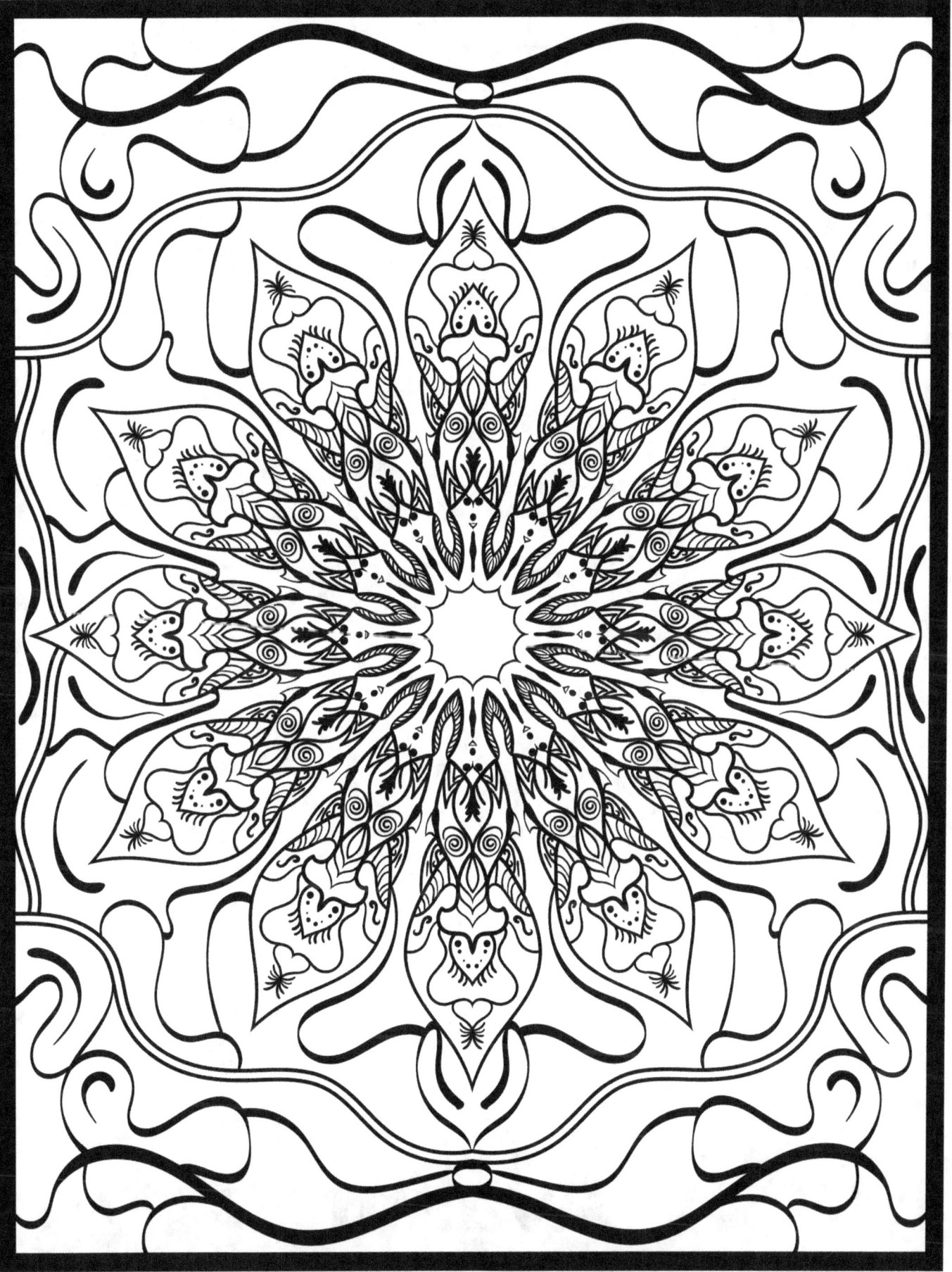

Avalon

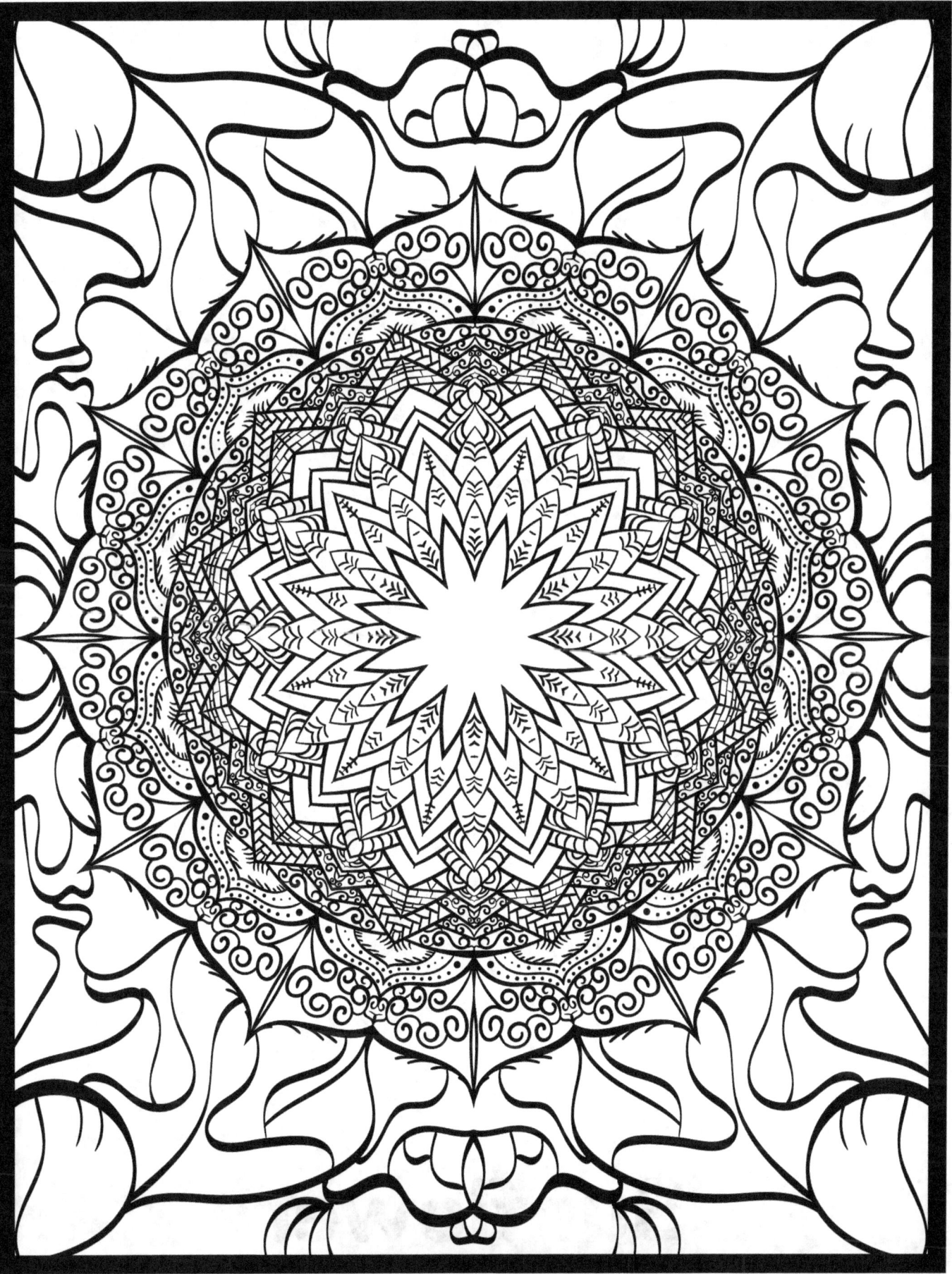

Sunflower

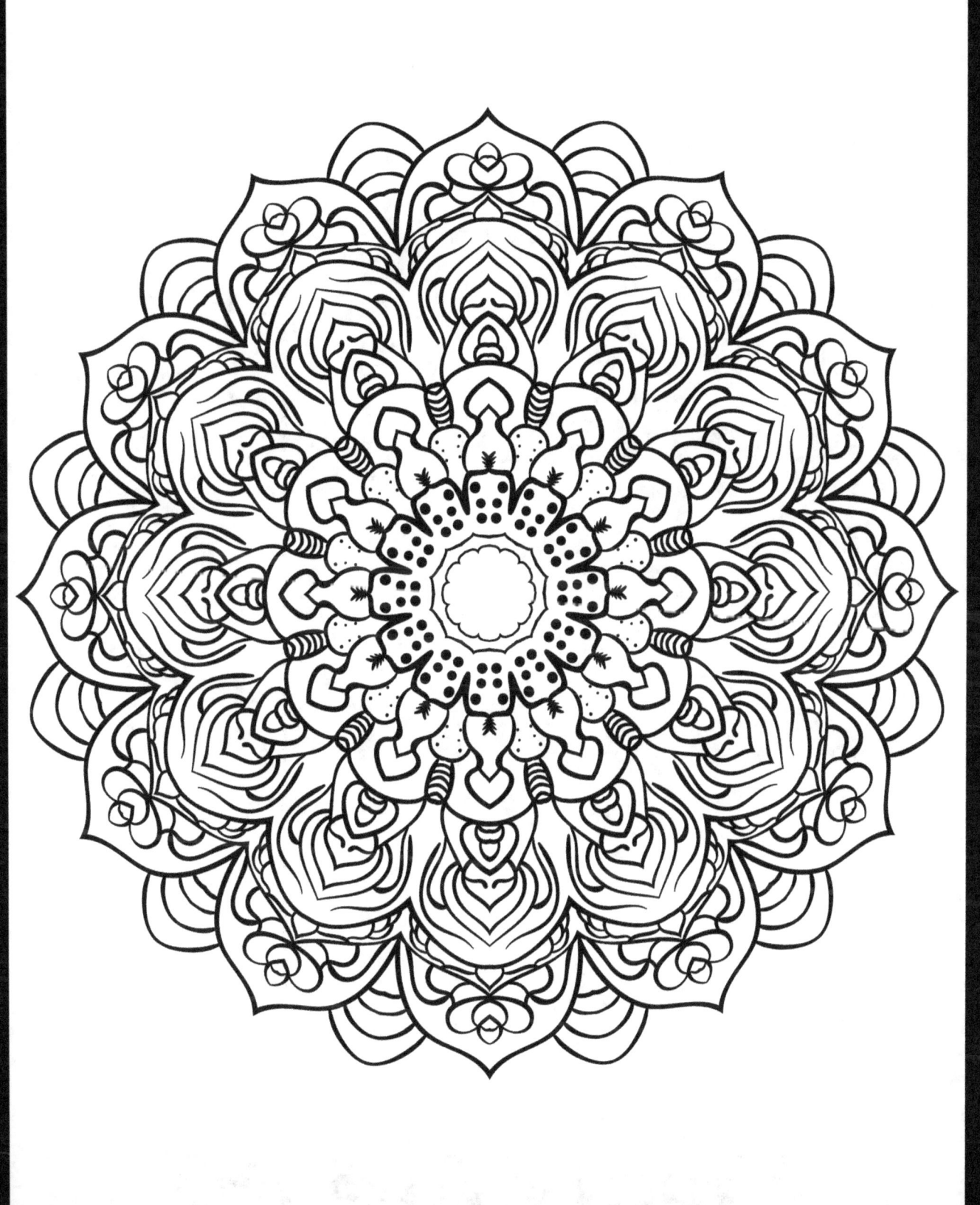

Empty Beauty

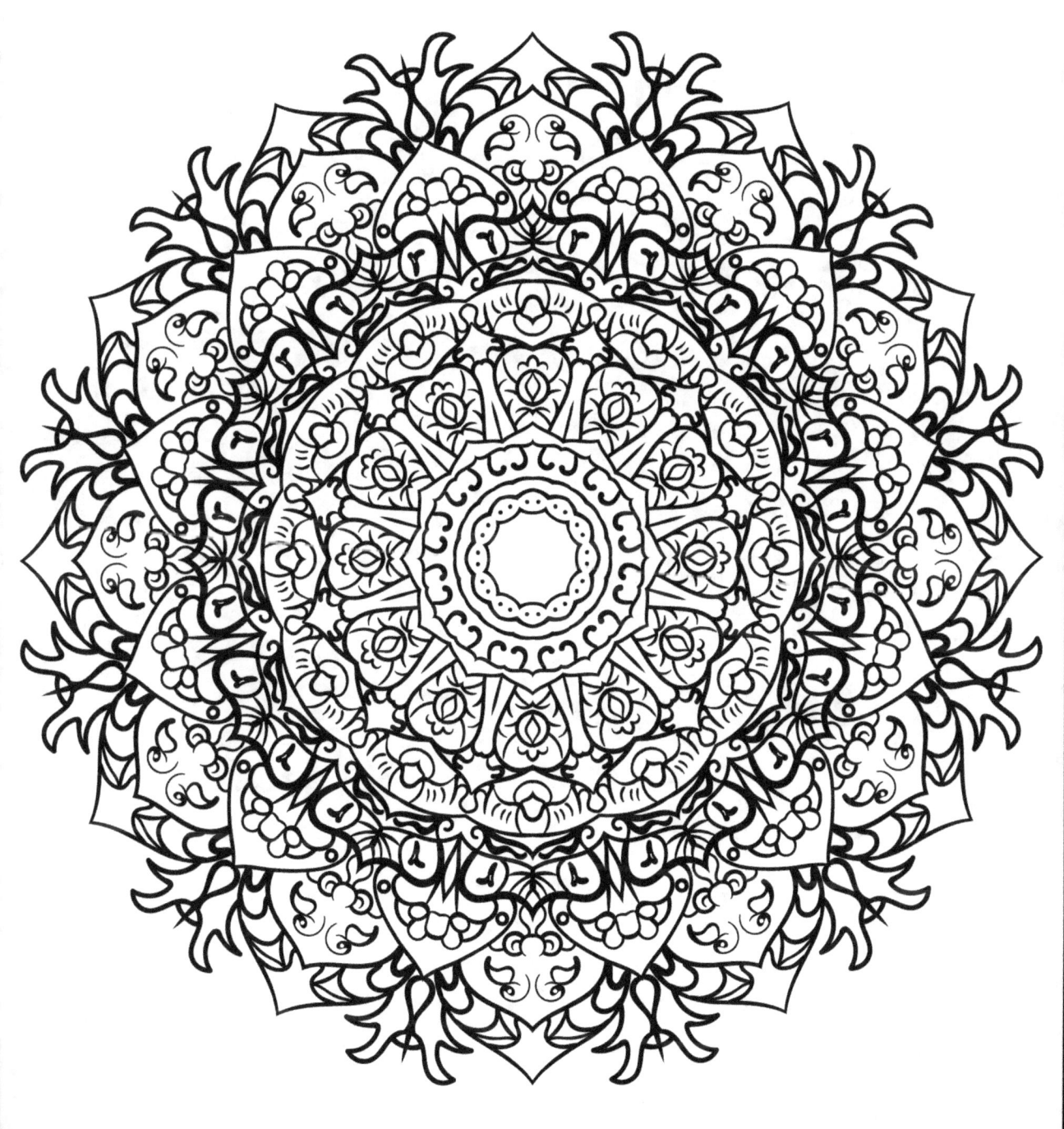

First Place

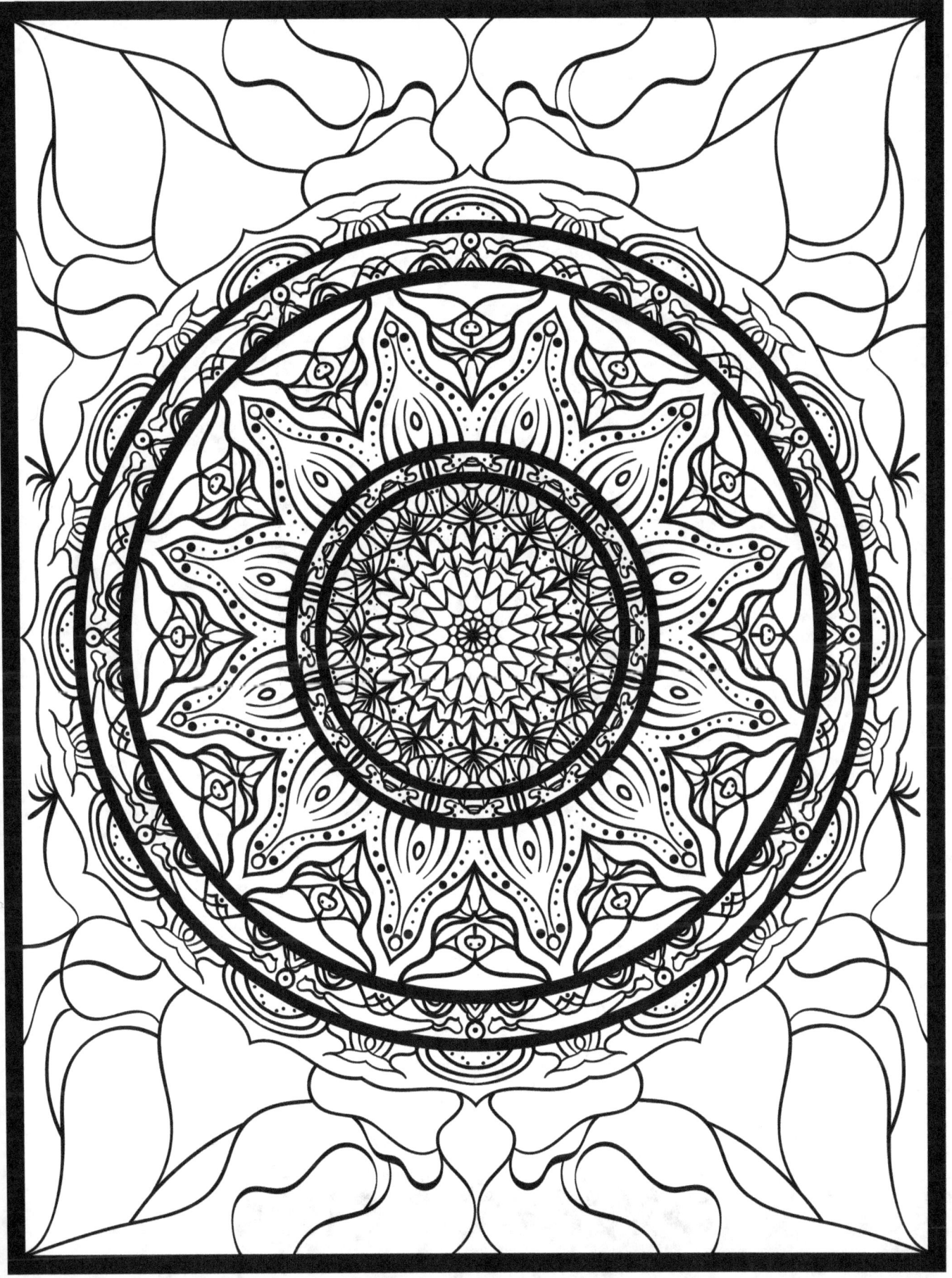

Sweet Fruit

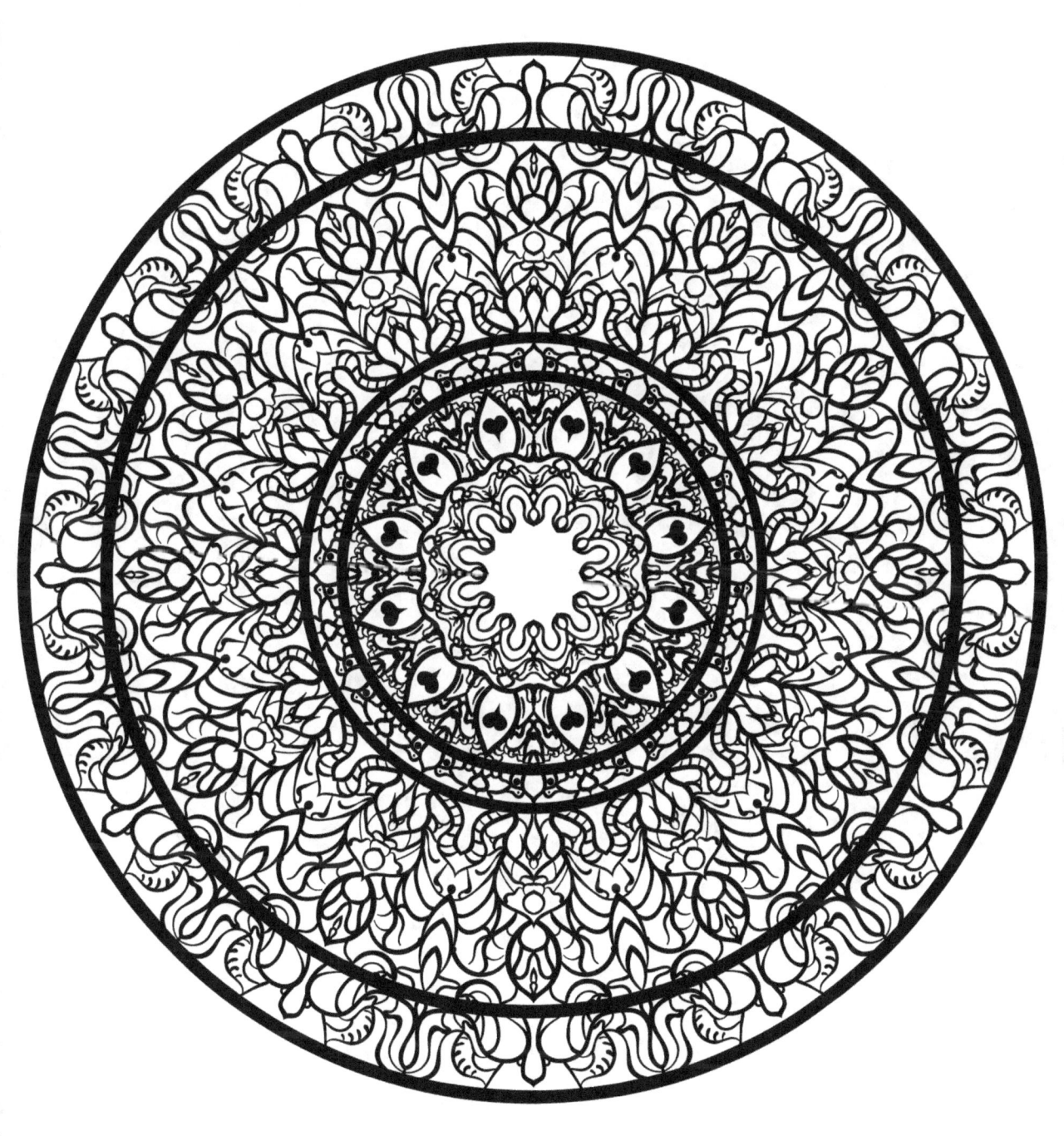

Love

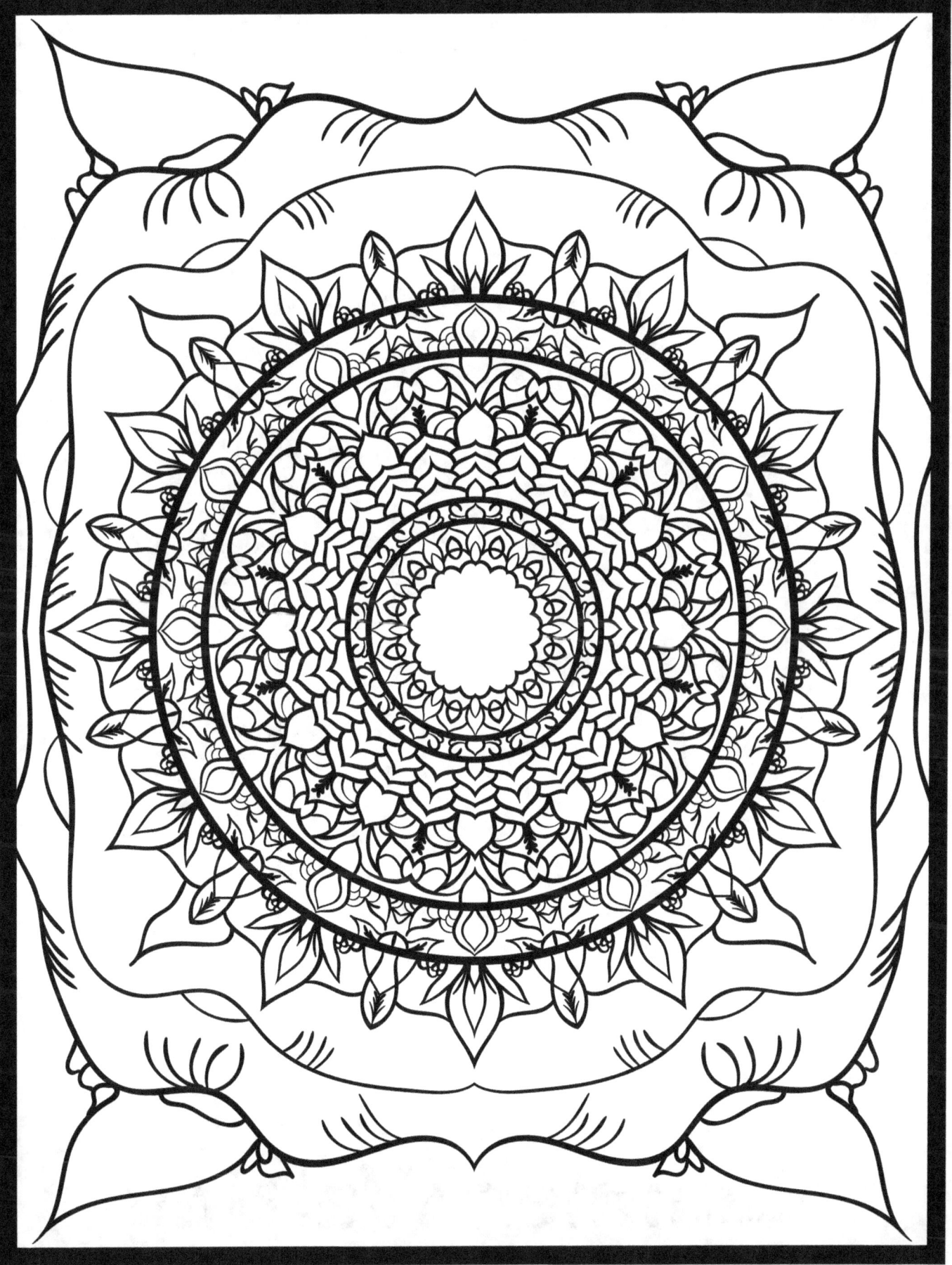

Summer Waiting

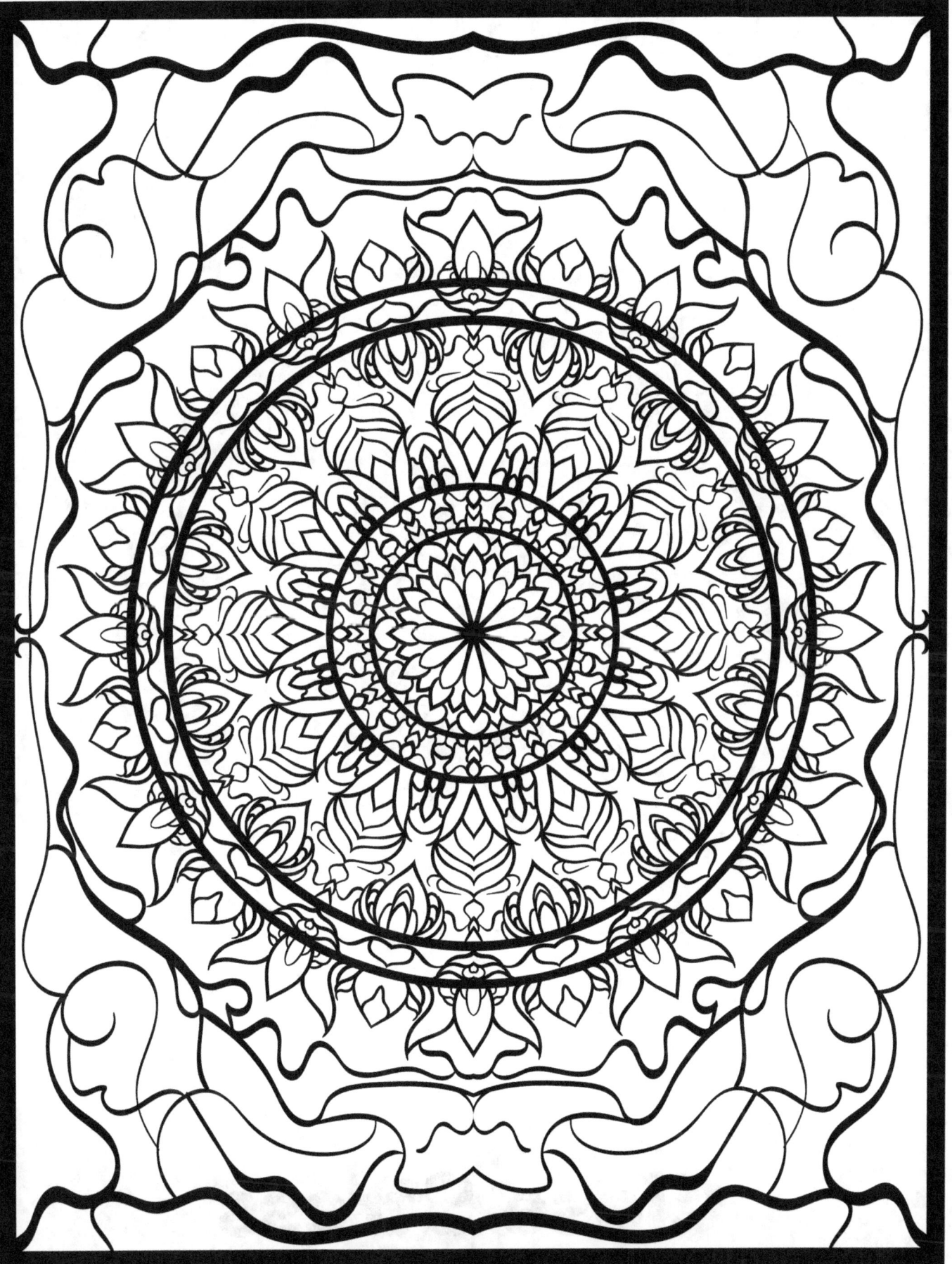

Close Stress

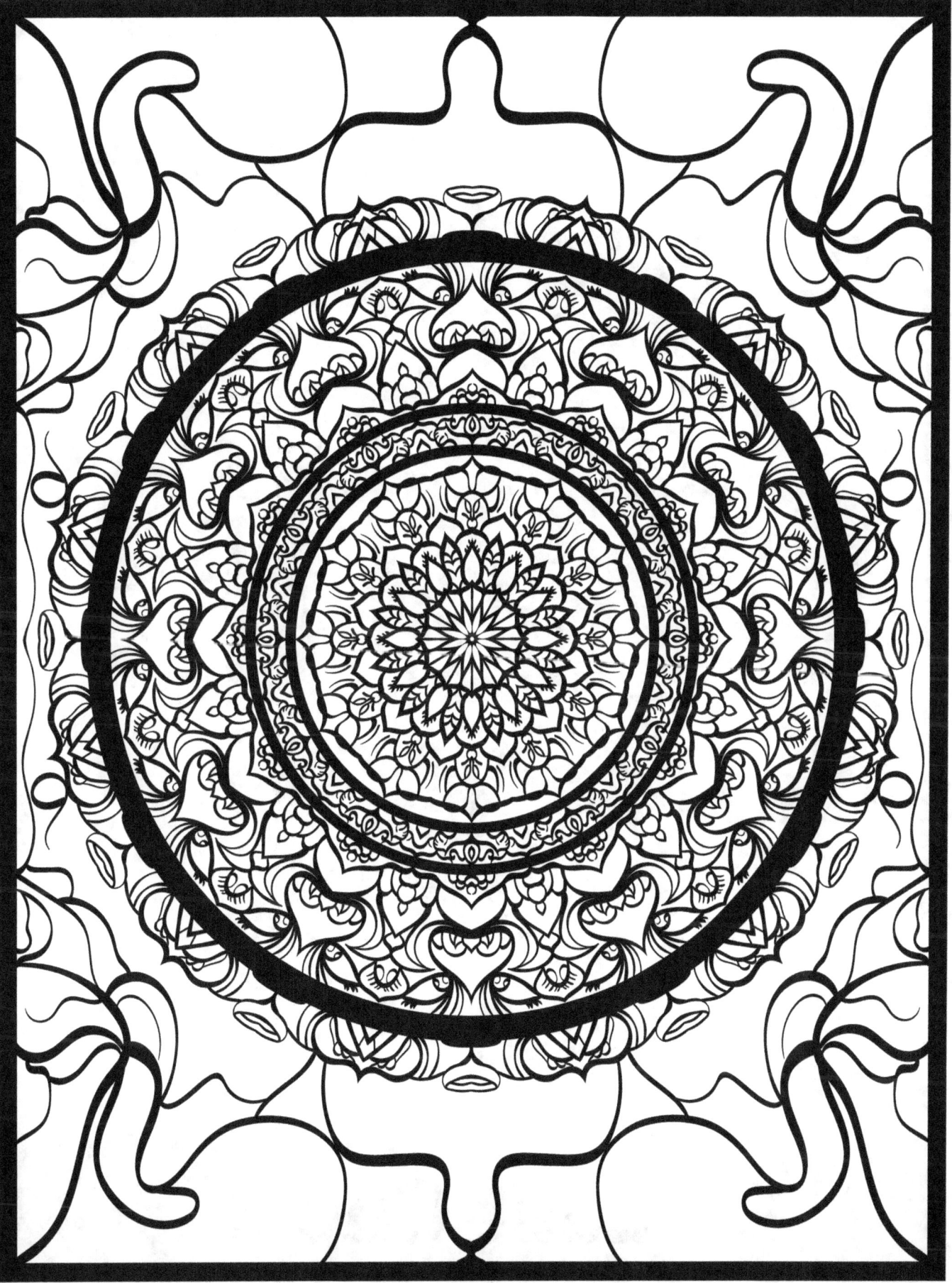

Last Cup

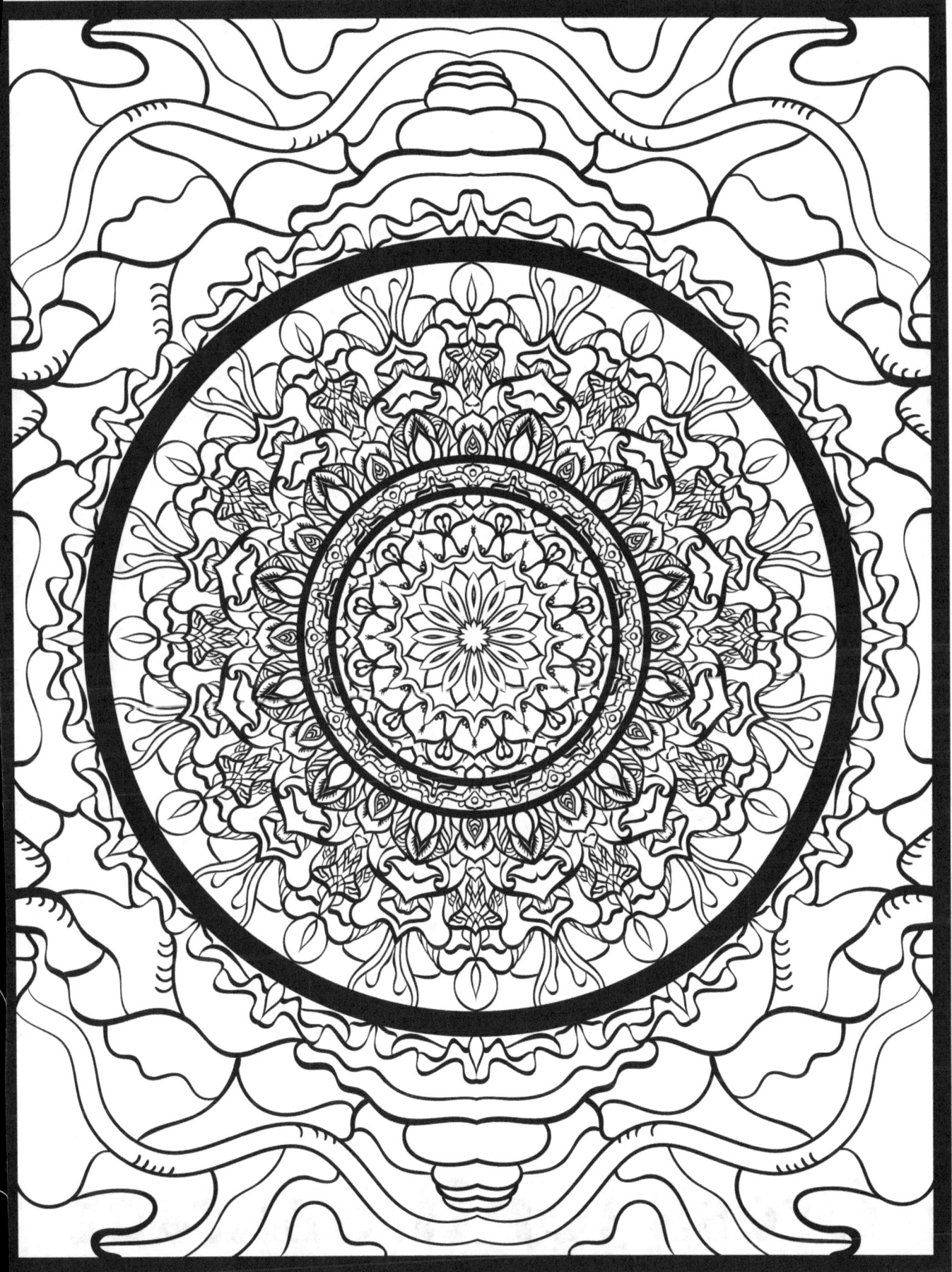

Dress for Breakfast